Education and Training 14–19

CURRICULUM, QUALIFICATIONS AND ORGANIZATION

Ann Hodgson and Ken Spours

Los Angeles • London • New Delhi • Singapore • Washington DC

© Ann Hodgson and Ken Spours 2008

First published 2008

Apart from any fair dealing for the purposes of research or private
study, or criticism or review, as permitted under the Copyright,
Designs and Patents Act, 1988, this publication may be
reproduced, stored or transmitted in any form, or by any means,
only with the prior permission in writing of the publishers, or in
the case of reprographic reproduction, in accordance with the
terms of licences issued by the Copyright Licensing Agency.
Enquiries concerning reproduction outside those terms should be
sent to the publishers.

SAGE Publications Ltd
1 Oliver's Yard
55 City Road
London EC1Y 1SP

SAGE Publications Inc.
2455 Teller Road
Thousand Oaks, California 91320

SAGE Publications India Pvt Ltd
B 1/I 1 Mohan Cooperative Industrial Area
Mathura Road
New Delhi 110 044

SAGE Publications Asia-Pacific Pte Ltd
33 Pekin Street #02–01
Far East Square
Singapore 048763

Library of Congress Control Number: 2008922941

British Library Cataloguing in Publication data

A catalogue record for this book is available from the British
Library

ISBN 978-84787-181-7
ISBN 978-84787-182-4 (pbk)

Typeset by Dorwyn, Wells, Somerset
Printed in Great Britain by Cromwell Press Ltd, Trowbridge, Wiltshire
Printed on paper from sustainable resources

EDUCATION AND TRAINING 14-19

contents

about the authors

Ann Hodgson has worked as a teacher, lecturer, LEA adviser, editor and civil servant, joining the Institute of Education, University of London in 1993, where she is now a Reader in Education and Faculty Director for Research, Consultancy and Knowledge Transfer. She is a co-director of the *Nuffield Review of 14–19 Education in England and Wales*, as well as a range of local authority and learning and skills council research and development projects related to institutional organization, governance and curriculum and qualifications reform. Ann has published widely on topics related to post-14 policy, lifelong learning and curriculum and qualifications reform.

Ken Spours is a Reader of Education, Head of the Department of Professional and Continuing Education and Director of the Centre for Post-14 Research and Innovation at the Institute of Education, University of London. Ken has researched the area of 14–19 education and training for two decades and has published numerous books, papers and journal articles on qualifications reform and education system performance. In 1990 he co-authored the influential Institute of Public Policy Research (IPPR) document *A British Baccalaureate*. He was also a member of the Tomlinson Working Group on 14–19 Reform in 2003–4 and is a director of the Nuffield Review of 14–19 Education and Training in England and Wales.

preface

The fact is that the world does move on and change and something that is achievable today simply may not have been yesterday. (PA 5)

A new volume on the reform of 14–19 education and training in England is badly needed. It will be the first research-based book looking at the 14–19 phase as a whole since the Government's rejection of the Tomlinson Report and the launch of its 14–19 White Paper in early 2005. This book is our attempt to provide an analysis of the position in 2008 and to offer ideas for the future, which were not deemed possible three years ago.

14–19 Education and Training: Curriculum, Qualifications and Organization seeks to communicate with, and to link, different communities involved in 14–19 reform – practitioners in schools, colleges and work-based learning, policy actors at national, regional and local levels and the academic community with its researchers, trainee teachers and students.

In doing so, the book takes a system-wide view as it describes, and tries to make sense of, a complex set of developments in the implementation stage of government policy. These include qualifications reform and the introduction of the Diplomas, changes in institutional arrangements and the formation of 14–19 Partnerships, the role of apprenticeships and the work-based route and debates about the future organization of 14–19 education and training in England.

We also try to give a voice to a range of policy actors, working in different parts of the system, who were interviewed as a source of evidence for the book. Their views on the 14–19 phase, government reforms and future possibilities were one of several sources of data we brought together to inform the book's seven chapters, and their quotes are coded (PA) plus their interview number. We also drew on findings from the *Nuffield Review of 14–19 Education and Training in England and Wales* and from an ESRC Teaching and Learning Research Programme project *The Impact of Policy on Learning and Inclusion in the Learning and Skills Sector*. Secondary sources included key government policy documents, academic and professional literature and press and web articles.

Our starting point is to question the rationale for a 14–19 phase – we do not take it as a given. However, in weighing up the evidence, early in the book we suggest that there are strong arguments for an extended upper secondary phase in England. Nevertherless, we are not convinced that current government policy will be able to produce a strong, inclusive and coherent 14–19 education and training system for all young people. Hence our argument that a 14–19 phase in England still remains largely a 'policy aspiration'.

While the book is research-based, it is also informed by debates about a more inclusive and unified approach to 14–19 education and training, which have been part of professional thinking since the late-1980s. This perspective is reflected in different ways across the seven chapters, but our central argument is that a strong and inclusive 14–19 phase should build on the strengths of the English system – bottom-up curriculum innovation, diverse approaches to pedagogy and its offer of a 'second chance' post-16 – while also addressing deep-seated problems. In making this argument, the book takes a critical view of policy that perpetuates the academic/vocational divide; competitive institutional relations; employer voluntarism; and top-down politically imposed agendas. We criticise, in particular, an approach to policy that does not provide an explicit long-term vision and does not draw adequately on professional expertise.

Chapter 1 lays out the rationale for a 14–19 phase, but also highlights the difficulties of realising it in the English context. This chapter uses the lens of international comparison to reflect on the main features, strengths and weaknesses of the English system. In Chapter 2 we provide an historical framework through which to understand how the current distinctive English approach to 14–19 has emerged. In doing this, we focus on the major debates around curriculum, qualifications and organization that have taken place over the last 20 years. In particular, we explain the ongoing controversy about the Government's rejection of the Tomlinson proposals for a unified diploma system. Chapters 3, 4 and 5 describe and analyse the three separate tracks that structure the 14–19 phase: general/academic; broad vocational; and work-based learning. Institutional and governance arrangements, including the emerging 14–19 Partnerships, constitute the focus of Chapter 6.

The final chapter lays out possible future directions for reform. We describe three positions. The Government's stance is characterized as 'pragmatic track-based', because its choice-based 14–19 agenda could be seen to lead to a reformulated triple-track system. The second position is taken by what we term 'pragmatic unifiers'. They believe that a broad local interpretation of the national reforms and trying to 'make the Diplomas work' will eventually produce a more unified system. As 'systemic unifiers', we take a third position, in which we argue for the need to view 14–19 education and training within its broader historical and system context. From this position, we argue for a triple shift involving the mutual reform of general and vocational education; the reinforcement of qualifications reform by the creation of 'strongly collaborative local learning systems' and by a more devolved and deliberative policy process that provides spaces for regional and local innovation within a national framework.

acknowledgements

We would like to acknowledge the help and support we received from the Nuffield Foundation and our colleagues on the Nuffield 14–19 Review of Education and Training in England and Wales – Geoff Hayward, Ewart Keep, Richard Pring, Gareth Rees and Stephanie Wilde – in researching this book. It was made much more possible too by the one term's study leave we were granted by the Institute of Education, University of London.

We are also grateful to the following for commenting on early drafts of chapters: Tony Breslin, Stuart Gardner, Maggie Greenwood, Sue Hawthorne, Geoff Hayward, Jeremy Higham, Tina Isaacs, Ewart Keep, David Raffe, Geoff Stanton, Gordon Stobart and Lorna Unwin.

In addition, we would like to thank the 23 people, representing a wide range of national, regional and local stakeholders and policy actors, who were prepared to be interviewed for this book and provided us with a rich background to 14–19 policy and practice. Particular thanks go to Richard Steer, who organized and participated in the interview process and read through the penultimate version of the whole book to check for consistency.

As usual we want to recognize the patience and tolerance of our families while we were writing this book.

Finally, we are grateful for the encouragement and practical advice we received from Marianne Lagrange and Matthew Waters from Sage.

chapter 1

DISCUSSING A 14–19 PHASE IN ENGLAND

14–19 EDUCATION AND TRAINING – IMPORTANT BUT POORLY UNDERSTOOD

Currently, 14–19 education in England is a paradox. It has become a prime area of policy development backed by serious resources aimed at improving national educational performance. It is a highly charged area with passionate debate amongst educationalists, policy-makers and the education research communities about how it should be organized and developed. At the same time, the majority of those outside the education system do not readily recognize the concept of a 14–19 phase (Lumby and Foskett 2005).

So why is something that is so important to policy-makers and educationalists not obvious to the general public? One major reason is that, despite the Government's recent announcement about raising the participation age to 18 by 2015 (DCSF 2007a), for all young people in England there is still a clear break at the age of 16 with the conclusion of compulsory education. At this point, they will either remain within a school sixth form to study to advanced level or will leave to go to a further education (FE) or sixth form college, enter an apprenticeship or even find themselves a job. Presently, 50 per cent of young people switch institution at 16 (DfES 2007a) and even those who remain at school see the sixth form as a new and distinctive learning environment (Gardner 2007). Moreover, the curriculum and the qualifications that young people take are also structured around a 16+ divide (Higham 2003). The National Curriculum ends at 16 when the vast majority of young people take General Certificate of Secondary Education (GCSE) qualifications, and their success in these examinations determines their choices post-16. Compared internationally, the English post-16 system is then highly specialized. In general education, learners study only three or four subjects at General Certificate of Education Advanced Level (A Level). Those taking vocational qualifications will normally focus on one occupational or sectoral area and, for many, these courses will be seen as distinctive from school and offering a fresh start (Coffield et al. 2008). So, both in terms of organization and of curriculum and qualifications, the learner experience is of break and difference rather than of continuity and progression 14–19.

In this chapter we outline a rationale for a 14–19 phase. This is followed by a description of the four features that shape the English system – participation and achievement, curriculum and qualifications, organization and governance and the influence of the labour market, employers and higher education. These specific national characteristics are then viewed within an international context, which demonstrates different possibilities for 14–19 policy. The chapter concludes by suggesting that current government policy has not confronted the historical English system features that work against the creation of a strong and visible 14–19 phase.

Arguments for a 14–19 phase

Given these circumstances, why have policy-makers and educationalists argued in favour of a 14–19 phase since the mid-1980s? We would suggest that there has been one leading reason, which is the need to encourage higher levels of participation in post-compulsory education and training as part of the drive for skills development and economic competitiveness and greater social cohesion (for example, DfES 2005a). England has traditionally trailed behind its major international competitors in this area and still continues to do so, a fact recognized by both researchers and policy-makers (for example Green and Steedman 1993; DfES 2001a; Leitch 2006). The most recent focus on 14–19 as a policy priority was given momentum by the revelation in 2003 that the UK languished 25th out of 29 countries in terms of the participation rates of 17-year-olds (DfES 2003). There is broad agreement that early school leaving with a youth labour market that attracts young people into low-skilled employment has been and remains an issue (Finegold and Soskice 1988; National Skills Task Force 2000; Hayward et al. 2005). The creation of a 14–19 phase, which spans compulsory and post-compulsory education could be seen, therefore, as England's answer to a historic problem of low post-16 participation.

The second reason relates to young people themselves. Drawing on studies related to 14–19-year-olds (for example, Blatchford 1996; De Pear 1997; Bentley 1998; Hodgson and Spours 2001), Lumby and Foskett suggest that they increasingly wish to 'control their lives, to receive respect from other adults, to make choices according to their own preferences and not necessarily to be confined by school parameters' (2005: 6). Lumby and Foskett use this as an argument for a distinctive phase of transition that reaches down into compulsory education and extends beyond school into further study and working life. In the context of this phase of education, the Nuffield Review of 14–19 Education and Training in England and Wales has posed the question: 'What constitutes an educated nineteen year old in this day and age?' The Review suggests that there is a set of knowledge, skills and attributes that all young people should acquire to become the citizens of the future (Hayward et al. 2006).

In the eyes of policy-makers, education practitioners and researchers, these reasons provide a strong rationale for a coherent 14–19 phase. However, at this point the consensus breaks down. There are sharply different views about how 14–19 education and training in England should be organized (for example Working Group on 14–19 Reform 2004a; DfES 2005a) given the fact that, at any one time, there are over three million 14–19-year-olds from different social and racial backgrounds, with different education histories and different aspirations.[1] Over the last two decades, there has been a major debate as to how common or differentiated young peoples' experience of 14–19 education and training should be in a phase in which 'staying in or moving class is most crucially negotiated' (Lumby and Foskett, 2005: 10).

As Chapter 2 will show, the dominant view, held by both Conservative and New Labour Governments, is that the creation of a 14–19 phase in England is about developing a vocational alternative to academic education. On the other hand, the view held by large sections of the education professional, policy, and research communities is that 14–19 education and training is about transforming learning for all young people. These differing visions have become crystallized around a series of debates, which can be seen to fall into three broad categories: curriculum and qualifications; organization and governance; work-based learning and the labour market. Examples of contested areas include whether the 14–19 phase should be based on an academic/vocational divide or a more unified curriculum and qualifications approach; whether institutional arrangements should be competitive or collaborative; and whether voluntarism in relation to employers and the labour market should be replaced by a more social partnership approach. We will return to these debates throughout the book. Here, we begin our discussion by outlining the main features of 14–19 education and training in England and then examining these through the lens of international comparison.

DESCRIBING THE ENGLISH 14–19 SYSTEM

There are a number of key features that affect the shape of 14–19 education and training in England and the role it plays in young peoples' lives. These include patterns and modes of participation and achievement; the role of qualifications and which ones young people take; where they study; how the system is organized and governed; and the shaping influence of employers, the labour market and higher education.

Participation and achievement

When compared internationally, England has been described as a 'medium participation and medium achievement system' (Hodgson and Spours 2000) and this picture broadly pertains in 2008. In 2006, 77 per cent of 16–18-year-olds were in some form of education and training, leaving just under a quarter not engaged with formal study. Moreover, as Figure 1.1 shows, participation in education and training drops off markedly at 17 and 18.

Within the overall level of participation, Figure 1.2 shows that full-time education is the dominant mode of participation post-16. It has remained broadly static over the last decade, but with a slight increase in the last couple of years. However, the recent modest increase in full-time participation has been cancelled out by a decline in the role of work-based learning and employer-funded training. The net result is that participation levels in 2006 are broadly the same as they were in the mid-1990s.

Of those 16–18-year-olds who remained in full-time education in 2006 (61 per cent), two-thirds were taking advanced level courses[2] with a tiny proportion (2 per cent) on advanced apprenticeships (DfES 2007b). Significantly more post-16 learners were studying in FE and sixth form colleges (30 per cent of all 16–18-year-olds) than in maintained and independent schools (23 per cent) (DfES 2007a). These key statistics, taken together, illustrate some of the salient features of the English system. It is education-based, predominantly full-time, with a very small work-based route and a strong role for colleges in post-compulsory education. Initial

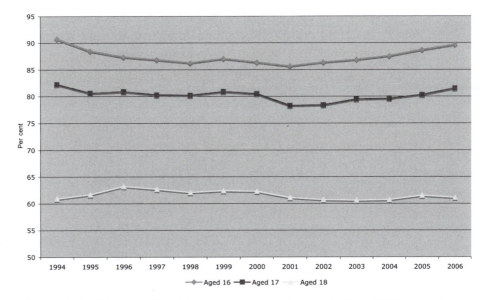
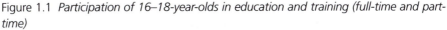

Figure 1.1 *Participation of 16–18-year-olds in education and training (full-time and part-time)*
Source: DfES Statistical First Release 22/2007 (DfES 2007a)

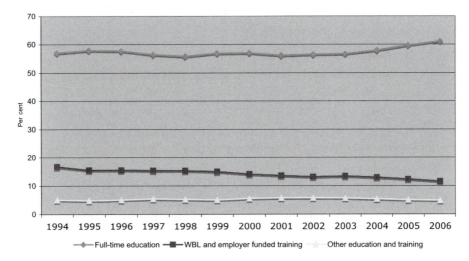

Figure 1.2 *Modes of participation of 16–18-year-olds in England*
Source: DfES Statistical First Release 22/2007 (DfES 2007a)

post-compulsory participation at 16 is relatively high, but is not sustained at 17 and 18, when the youth labour market exerts an increasing pull. In addition, there is a steady rise in the number of those not involved in education, employment or training (or NEET) from 10 per cent at the age of 16 to just under 15 per cent at the age of 18 in 2006 (DfES 2007b).

Overall, full- and part-time participation rates have not risen significantly since the mid-1990s, fuelling concerns amongst policy-makers that the country may find itself at a disadvantage when compared internationally (DIUS 2007). Hence the recent policy announcement about using legislation to raise the participation age to 17 in 2010 and 18 in 2015 (DCSF 2007a).

However, as Figure 1.3 shows, attainment rates in GCSEs and A Levels have improved steadily over the last 10 years. Since 2001, the A Level pass rate has been boosted by the *Curriculum 2000* reforms. Since 2004, the attainment of 5 A*–C GCSEs has been increased by the inclusion of GCSE equivalent applied/vocational qualifications.

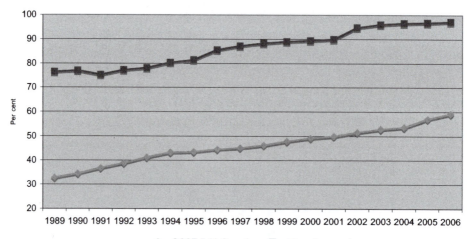

Figure 1.3 *Attainment of GCSE five A*–C grades and A Level passes*
Source: Tables 18 and 23, *Education Briefing Book* (IOD 2007)

The proportion of 16-year-olds gaining five GCSEs at grades A*–C (or equivalent) reached just under 60 per cent in 2006, although the proportion of those reaching this benchmark including English and Maths was much lower at 46 per cent (DfES 2007b).[3] At advanced level, pass rates in A Levels and Advanced Vocational Certificates of Education (AVCEs) have risen from 77 per cent in 1989 to 97 per cent in 2006 (IOD 2007), with 68 per cent gaining grades A–C (DfES 2007c) (see Chapter 3 for more detail). Statistics are compiled differently for vocational courses in FE and for work-based learning. In both these cases, 'success rates'[4] have improved significantly over the last five years. In FE colleges for 16–18-year-olds, they have risen from 64 per cent in 2001/2 to 75 per cent in 2005/6, and for 16–18-year-old apprenticeships from 27 per cent in 2001/2 to 54 per cent in 2005/6 (LSC 2007). These improvements notwithstanding, attainment in vocational learning remains considerably lower than that in general education.

What these statistics cannot adequately explain is the stark differences between the educational experiences of 14–19-year-olds in the current English education and training system. Young people who do well at school and gain good grades at GCSE (for example five or more passes at grades A*–C) have all post-16 options open to them, although they are most likely to remain in full-time education either in a school sixth form or sixth form college and to take A Levels. For those who fail to reach this GCSE threshold, post-16 options are limited to vocational qualifications below advanced level (the majority of which will be offered in FE colleges), or to a variety of training programmes, such as Entry to Employment (Hayward et al. 2005). As one of our interviewees observed: 'Huge numbers of people emerge out of this system now believing still that "education and training are not for the likes of me" – de-motivated and dysfunctional' (PA 15).[5]

High attaining learners are more likely to make a seamless transition in the 14–19 phase with many simply remaining in their 11–18 school for the whole of this period, while low-attainers have to negotiate a complex set of curricular and institutional transitions (Stanton and Fletcher 2006). However, many of the latter are willing to do this because of disaffection with the school system and the opportunities that further education (FE) colleges and work-based learning provide for a second chance (Coffield et al. 2008).

Curriculum and qualifications

Qualifications play a fundamental shaping role in the English 14–19 system, but the role of curriculum is much weaker. Qualifications define what learners study, how they are assessed and, in many cases, determine how they are taught (Ecclestone 2007). The English system has a National Curriculum at the beginning of the 14–19 phase. It ensures a core of common curricular experiences for all learners up to the age of 16, comprising English, mathematics, science, ICT, physical education, citizenship, work-related learning and enterprise, and religious, personal social, health and careers education. While on first sight this appears quite a broad curriculum, in international terms it is narrow. Since 2002 and the publication of the Government's 14–19 Green Paper (DfES 2002), 14–16-year-olds no longer have to study a modern foreign language, the arts, humanities or design and technology, although these have to be on offer to them should they wish to continue with them up to the age of 16. The accent in policy has been on flexibility, choice and 'personalization' throughout the 14–19 phase, with a very limited common entitlement for post-16 learners, which only extends to functional English, Mathematics and ICT, although these are not compulsory. Compared internationally, two things stand out in relation to the English 14–19 curriculum. First, it is difficult to continue in general education post-16 unless you achieve the benchmark of 5 A*–C grades at GCSE. Second, there is a very limited notion of curricular breadth post-16 both for those taking A Levels and for those taking a vocational route. This has been a source of controversy for at least two decades.

The corollary to a weak curriculum approach to 14–19 education and training is the strength of the qualifications hierarchy. There is a perverse synergy between general and vocational qualifications, with the former always 'shaping' the latter (see Chapters 3 and 4). An interviewee highlighted the system 'pull' of A Levels: 'As long as you've got something as a Gold Standard with the A Levels, everything else that you're going to do is going to be judged in terms of how closely it aligns with them' (PA 9). The culture of the 14–19 phase is, therefore, determined by A Levels and GCSEs, which are not only numerically dominant (virtually all 14–16 learners take one or more GCSEs and 40 per cent of 16–19-year-olds take two or more A Levels – DfES 2007a), but also politically totemic. A Levels have a history going back nearly 60 years and GCSEs are seen as the direct descendants of O Levels, which still persist in the public imagination.

Vocational qualifications for 14–19-year-olds, on the other hand, are much newer, suffer from constant reform and name change, either as a result of government policy or by private awarding bodies attempting to sell a new product (see Chapter 5).[6] As we have seen, they are taken by a much smaller number of young people, are viewed as 'alternatives' to mainstream A Levels and GCSEs and are primarily associated with lower achievers and FE colleges. As a leading educational commentator put it: 'vocational education – a great idea for other people's children' (Wolf 2002).

The purposes, pedagogy and assessment regimes are very different in general and vocational qualifications (Ecclestone 2002). In the former, the dominant features are preparation for higher study, subject and theoretical knowledge and external assessment, with an accent on selection and rationing (Young 1998). Vocational qualifications, on the other hand, are primarily designed for preparation for work or higher-level occupational study at advanced level, although, at the lower levels, they have also been used by government for social inclusion purposes (Keep 2005a; Fuller and Unwin 2003).

14–19 qualifications have thus become a site of social competition and even constitute a 'social battleground' (Lumby and Foskett 2005), as they divide young people and social groups (Clarke 2007) and increase social inequality, a process exacerbated by the market reforms of school and college finances (Machin and Vignoles 2006).

Organization and governance

The English institutional landscape has become more complex over the last 20 years as a result of both Conservative and New Labour policy to increase choice and competition (Hayward et al. 2005, 2006). The 14–19 phase is not delivered by dedicated 14–19 institutions. Instead there is a 'mixed economy' of providers: 11–16 schools, 11–18 maintained and independent schools, sixth form colleges, local authority controlled sixth form centres, skills centres and academies, general FE colleges, tertiary colleges, City Technology Colleges, new academies, independent training providers and, of course, employers. Even the *Building Schools for the Future* initiative has not fully acknowledged the 14–19 phase and its need for area-based planning.

The result is that, in institutional terms, the 14–19 phase does not exist in any meaningful sense. Not only is there a sharp institutional break at 16+, but this is compounded by curricular and qualifications division, in which different providers deliver different balances of academic and vocational programmes. The effects of this division and complexity are felt most acutely by those learners who fail to achieve five A*–C grades at GCSE and who are often forced to leave school at 16 in order to access vocational learning (Hodgson and Spours 2006a). One of our interviewees highlighted the unfairness of this: 'I've always thought that the most vulnerable young people are the ones that don't need to be told at 16 "you have to go elsewhere because the school doesn't cater for post-16" or to be told at 16 that "actually, the school doesn't want you at 16 thank you very much, we're focusing on A Levels"' (PA 10). Moreover, as we will discuss in greater detail in Chapter 6, competition between schools and between schools and colleges makes the provision of impartial guidance for young people difficult to achieve.

The Government's response to this complex institutional picture has been to face two ways simultaneously. On the one hand, it has promoted institutional diversity as part of its choice-based broader public service reform agenda (PMSU 2006, 2007). On the other, it has exhorted providers to collaborate to meet the requirements of its newly established 14–19 Entitlement[7] and, in particular, to give learners access to the new 14–19

Diplomas (DfES 2005a, 2005b) – see Chapters 4 and 6 for more detail.

While 14–19 institutional arrangements work against the concept of a 14–19 phase, recent government policy has attempted to reform governance arrangements to develop a more coherent approach to funding, planning, guidance and inspection. In 2007, the Department for Education and Skills was split into two new ministries: the Department for Children, Schools and Families (DCSF) and the Department for Innovation, Universities and Skills (DIUS). The former has responsibility, amongst other things, for 14–19 education and training. Moreover, from 2010, local authorities (LAs) will fund, plan and co-ordinate the 14–19 phase at local level, a role which has been shared with the Learning and Skills Council (LSC). The Common Inspection Framework now covers all education and training provision for 14–19-year-olds as a result of the merger between the Office for Standards in Education (Ofsted) and the Adult Learning Inspectorate (ALI) in 2006. The Connexions service, which is responsible for the well-being and guidance of young people, was brought back under LA control (DfES 2006a). However, LAs do not have jurisdiction over FE colleges, which are independent corporations, nor over independent schools, academies, trust schools, training providers or employers. Some LAs are very small and, as we explore in more detail in Chapter 6, powers invested in them may not be equal to their responsibilities.

Unless this changes, LAs will not be in a position to create a more coherent 14–19 institutional system out of a complex mosaic of competing interests. In the current context of national policy supporting institutional competition and a weakly planned local landscape, 14–19 institutional arrangements may actively be fuelling social and racial segregation. Recent research suggests that school sixth forms and sixth form colleges cater mainly for Level 3 and white British learners, while colleges of general education take the majority of Entry Level 1 and Level 2 post-16 learners and a higher proportion of Black and ethnic minority groups (Stanton and Fletcher 2006).

INFLUENCE OF THE LABOUR MARKET, EMPLOYERS AND HIGHER EDUCATION

The youth labour market has played a defining role in the 14–19 education and training system in England, because it has been a major factor in determining post-16 participation patterns (Ashton and Green 1996; Hayward et al. 2006). On the other hand, employers are noted for their relative lack of involvement in the provision of apprenticeships (see Chapter 5) and their 'curious absence' in relation to the education and training system as a whole (Keep 2005a). Government policy in this area has been noted for its voluntarist approach and the lack of a regulatory framework to promote employer engagement (Hayward et al. 2006). The effects of a relatively marginal role of employers in the organization and provision of the 14–19 phase has not allowed the work-based route to flourish and to provide high-quality vocational learning for large numbers of young people (Nuffield Review 2008a, 2008b). This vacuum has had to be filled by FE colleges, independent training providers and government initiatives, such as Young Apprenticeships and Entry to Employment. Despite employers' relative lack of engagement, their voice is privileged by government in an attempt to make the 14–19 phase more 'employer-led' (for example DIUS 2007) and has been influential in shaping government policy, not only on vocational qualifications but also on GCSEs and A Levels (see Chapters 2 and 3).

Higher education providers have a long history of shaping secondary and post-16 education (Wilde and Wright 2007) and their influence on an emerging 14–19 phase is as strong as ever because they control entry to sought-after university places (Lumby and Foskett 2005). With this power, universities affected the course of the *Curriculum 2000* advanced level reforms in England (Hodgson et al. 2005a). In the context of a 50 per cent higher education participation target, universities are being courted by government to support the new 14–19 Diplomas (see Chapter 4). Some vice-chancellors have even been recruited as 'Diploma champions' (DfES 2006b) and a number have been given a role in designing these qualifications.

In summary, it is possible to argue that the weight of historical arrangements continues to work against a strong 14–19 system. One of our interviewees put it more starkly: 'I mean it's only a construct when all's said and done. There isn't a 14–19 phase. It's split in the middle ... it's an assertion of existence from the centre' (PA10).

THE ENGLISH 14–19 SYSTEM VIEWED FROM A DISTANCE

At this point it is important to stand back from the detail of the English system to examine how far it reflects wider international trends. As Raffe argues, international comparison helps us to understand our own system better and to identify cross-national trends and pressures that affect all countries in order to ground policy options in a broader context (2007: 140). Green and colleagues (1999) remind us that policy-makers in different countries face common pressures and challenges but respond to these through their own national histories and traditions.

Wider international trends

In several important respects, the idea of a 14–19 phase in England broadly goes with the flow of international developments in what is termed 'upper secondary education'. This term is used to describe the phase that follows primary and lower secondary education. Le Metais (2002), in a study of international developments in upper secondary education, identified a number of common features of these systems, many of which England shares. These include a desire to increase participation up to the age of 18 or 19; the fostering of broad skills for employment, independent study and citizenship; softening the boundaries between general and vocational education; attempting to make learning and accreditation more flexible; concern to increase the number of learners studying mathematics and science; and greater accountability through more external assessment. In addition, Clarke and Winch (2007) point to the fact that apprenticeships are in decline across all European systems, leading to the need to provide more vocational education in schools and colleges. They also argue that European systems need to converge further in order to cope with large-scale migration, amongst other things.

Beyond these common features, it is possible to distinguish groups of countries which appear to share particular features. According to Green (2006), the UK upper secondary system broadly falls into what he terms the 'Anglo-Saxon model', along with the USA, Australia and New Zealand,[8] which are characterized by high levels of school diversity and regulation through quasi-market competition. He also notes that these governance features tend to reduce social mobility and increase social inequality in education.

There are, however, aspects of upper secondary education where England finds itself almost alone or sharing system features with a near neighbour. England and Wales are the only two countries that have decided to begin their upper secondary education phase at the age of 14. Commonly, upper secondary education systems begin at the age of 15 or 16, ending at 18 or 19. In terms of aims and purposes for the upper secondary phase, England's focus is narrow in comparison with other countries. It expresses the aims of 14–19 education almost exclusively in terms of choice and flexibility, a strategy designed to raise educational participation and performance. Other countries have a broader set of purposes. Sweden, for example, sees its upper secondary education 'helping students develop their personalities and an interest in culture and the humanities and providing the general education necessary to play a full and responsible role as citizens in a democratic society' (Le Metais 2002: 9). Pring argues that the absence of shared aims and values for the 14–19 phase in England is the result of policy-making being dominated by the 'limited concept of academic and vocational' (2007: 128) and by a general lack of vision. In addition, and crucially in terms of debates about 14–19, England is alone in not prescribing any core of compulsory learning beyond the age of 16. A related feature of the English system is that it does not have a common school leaving award to mark the end of the upper secondary phase. Most countries have some form of diploma based on a common core of subjects, a block of associated specialist learning and a range of electives, of which perhaps the most widely known are the French Baccalaureate, the US High School Graduation Diploma and the Irish Leaving Certificate (Le Metais 2002). Hence, one of the reasons for the recent debates about diplomas, graduation certificates and overarching awards in the English system (see Chapter 2).

Difference, however, does not automatically signal weakness. The English upper secondary system is judged to have some strengths. It is seen to be flexible, offering strong opportunities for 'second-chance learning' and to have a long-standing tradition of 'bottom-up' innovation (Raffe et al. 1998). These strengths are also reflections of its major weaknesses described earlier – its elective nature, which prevents breadth and strong common learning, the fact that its academic/vocational divide contributes to social segregation and that the upper secondary system is constantly remediating for learning failure in lower secondary education.

Home international comparisons – Scotland, Wales and Northern Ireland

In international comparison, the UK is often treated as a single unit of analysis. However, 'home international comparison' between England, Scotland, Wales and Northern Ireland reveals that countries which share important UK-wide features, such as labour markets and higher education institutions, can take different paths of development in the area of upper secondary education (Raffe 2007). A process of divergence has taken place, particularly following democratic devolution in Scotland and Wales in 1999 (Raffe 2006). Here, we briefly consider the different approaches taken to upper secondary education by the governments in Scotland, Wales and Northern Ireland.

Raffe (2007) suggests that policy-makers have key strategic choices to make about the organization of upper secondary education. They have to decide between a more 'track-based' (that is separate and distinctive vocational and academic pathways),[9] a more unified (that is a common learning and qualifications structure) or a more 'linkage' approach to qualifications frameworks (that is retention of separate tracks but increasing the links between them). They also need to make decisions about whether to develop a single phase of upper secondary education that straddles compulsory and post-compulsory education; how to structure progression and whether to opt for a more baccalaureate-type model or a more 'climbing frame' approach; as well as how to organize work-based provision.[10] Policy-makers in the four countries of the UK have adopted different approaches in these areas.

The Scottish *Higher Still* reforms began in 1999 with the introduction of new national qualifications covering all general and vocational courses in schools and colleges for learners beyond the age of 16. *Higher Still* has thus been described as a unified curriculum and qualifications framework for upper secondary education (Raffe et al. 2007), although this does not mean that all learners take a single diploma-type award. Instead, they pursue a range of both general and vocational modules within a single credit-based framework. Unlike England, Scotland has not adopted the concept of a distinct 14–19 phase. Since the publication of A *Curriculum for Excellence* (Scottish Executive 2004), the Scottish Government has emphasized the all-through nature of education 3–18, but with flexibility from 14+.

In some respects the Northern Ireland education system stands apart in having an 11+ examination, which selects students for either grammar or secondary modern schools, although this form of selection will be abolished from September 2008. However, in other respects, it is closer to England, being in the process of developing a 14–19 phase with an increasing focus on vocational provision and collaboration between schools (DENI 2007).

Wales shares some common features with the English system. Both countries organize upper secondary education in terms of a 14–19 phase with a policy focus on increasing rates of participation, achievement and progression through greater curricular choice, an emphasis on skills development and work-based learning, qualifications reform and a more personalized approach to learning, advice and guidance (WAG 2002; DfES 2005a). Wales also has 14–19 Networks of schools, colleges and work-based learning providers that broadly correspond to England's 14–19 Partnerships. However, in Wales, 14–19 curriculum and qualifications reform is articulated through a common framework entitled *Learning Pathways 14–19*. This comprises six key entitlements which, together, offer young people broad programmes of study combining formal qualifications, non-formal awards and informal experiences (WAG 2002: v). Learning Pathways will be accredited through the *Welsh Baccalaureate*, which is a single overarching award recognizing this wide range of qualifications and experiences. In comparison with England, therefore, Wales has moved decisively in a more unified direction and attempts to ensure breadth of learning throughout its 14–19 phase (see Hayward et al. 2006, Chapter 2, for more detail on the Welsh system).

What these brief vignettes of the three other UK systems demonstrate is that significant curricular and qualifications divergence is possible even though all four countries share a similar economic context. We will argue in the final chapter that it is important to use international comparisons when considering future policy directions in England. However, this aspiration needs to be tempered by the realization that there is no strong evidence to date that policy-makers are willing to engage in policy learning of this type (Raffe and Spours 2007).

CONCLUSION

In describing the English system through the lenses of international and home international comparison, we have noted a number of features that make it distinctive. Together with Wales, England is the only national system to describe its upper secondary phase in terms of the years that straddle compulsory and post-compulsory education. It is largely school- and college-based with a very small work-based route and low levels of employer engagement. Despite the fact that it has an 'integrated' institutional structure (that is, schools and FE colleges deliver both general and vocational education) it is, nevertheless, highly selective in terms of qualification pathways with a strong hierarchy between academic and vocational learning. Because of these features, there is a relatively narrow core curriculum 14–16 and no common core or clearly articulated overarching aims and purposes for the curriculum post-16. Moreover, unlike many other systems, there is no single award to mark the end of the upper secondary phase. Finally, institutional arrangements are highly marketized, which can be seen to compound curricular and qualifications divisions.

We started this chapter by suggesting that a 14–19 phase was important but largely hidden from view because of the sharp break at 16, which pervades the public psyche. Government policy has not yet addressed historic curricular, qualifications and institutional discontinuities despite the Government's focus on 14–19 policy since 2001. We will argue in this book that as a result, while a 14–19 phase is necessary, it is still exceedingly fragile and requires further reform.

NOTES

[1] This rough calculation for the phase as a whole is based on the number of 16-year-olds in 2006: 662,300 multiplied by five (DfES 2007a).

[2] In international terms, advanced level courses or Level 3 corresponds with qualifications required for entry to what the OECD refers to as 'tertiary level education' but what is called 'higher education' in England.

[3] GCSE equivalent includes GCSEs in applied subjects and General National Vocational Qualifications at Intermediate Level.

[4] Successful completion is defined by the number of learning aims achieved divided by the number of starters, excluding any learners who transferred onto another qualification within the same institution (LSC 2007).

[5] Between September and December 2007, with the help of Richard Steer, we interviewed a total of 23 policy actors (PA) involved in the 14–19 reform process. They included politicians, policy advisers, senior civil servants, academics, officials from national government agencies, awarding bodies and representatives of local authorities, teacher unions and professional associations and employers. We have used codes (PA 1–25) for interviewees and have not indicated the organization to which they belong in order to fully protect their identity. We realize that this limits the salience of some of the comments but it was necessary to respect interviewees' rights to anonymity so they could speak more freely. From these interviews, quotations have been selected for their illuminative powers but all interviews have been used as background information, triangulated with written sources.

[6] The English system is alone in having private awarding bodies, which are regulated by a non-departmental public body, the Qualifications and Curriculum Authority (QCA).

[7] All 14–16-year-olds are entitled to National Curriculum core subjects (English, mathematics and science), foundation subjects (ICT, PE, citizenship, work-related learning and enterprise, religious education, personal, social, health and careers education), all 17 Diplomas lines and to choose courses in the arts, design and technology and modern foreign languages. 16–19-year-olds are entitled to all 17 Diploma lines, and functional English, mathematics and ICT up to at least Level 2.

[8] We distinguish here between UK systems in which England, Scotland, Wales and Northern Ireland share important features (for example the labour market) and England-specific characteristics that affect 14–19 in particular, such as institutional organization and governance.

[9] We use the term 'academic' rather than 'general' when describing distinct qualifications tracks. The term 'track' refers to a qualification-led curriculum which has a distinctive content, assessment and mode of learning. It thus tends to channel learners in a particular direction, minimizing opportunities for flexible movement between different types of qualifications and curricula. We contrast the notion of a 'track' with the idea of a curriculum 'route or routeway' which allows learners to progress either horizontally or vertically. This is made possible when qualifications are less distinctive and share common properties in terms of assessment, knowledge and skills.

[10] By the term 'baccalaureate approach' we refer to the organization of learning and its accreditation through a grouped award, such as the International Baccalaureate, which stresses coherence and breadth. A 'climbing frame approach', on the other hand, is based on modular or unitized qualifications which allow learners more flexibility in terms of programme design and accumulating credit for progression.

chapter 2

UNDERSTANDING 14–19 – AN HISTORICAL AND POLITICAL FRAMEWORK

THE IMPORTANCE OF POLICY MEMORY

14–19 policy is both complex and contested, demanding what Higham and Yeomans (2007a) refer to as 'policy memory'. By this they mean the way in which policy actors use or do not use the history of past policies to reflect on current policy. They argue that the education policy community in England has experienced a collective policy amnesia, which results in them revisiting policies that have failed in the past. This chapter is a deliberate attempt to exercise policy memory in order to understand the main forces shaping 14–19 education and training in England, why there are sharply differing views about current policy, how mistakes might be avoided and the way in which policy needs to develop in the future.

Looking back over the last 20 years, it could be argued that the concept of 14–19 has arisen as a response to particular problems, rather than as something 'natural' to the English education and training system. Many in the education profession, including ourselves, have seen a 14–19 phase as a way of reducing the deep curricular and organizational divisions at 16+ (for example AoC et al. 1997). Others, particularly in the national policy community, are more tolerant of division, stress the need for greater choice at the age of 14 and look to a range of vocational alternatives to GCSEs and A Levels to ensure all young people remain in education and training until the age of 18/19 (for example DfES 2005a). Despite passionate talk about the intrinsic importance of 14–19 education and training (for example Working Group on 14–19 Reform 2004a; DfES 2005a; Lumby and Foskett 2005), the idea of a 14–19 phase could thus be seen as a form of responsiveness. The 14–19 concept has manifested itself in different ways over the past two decades, has ebbed and flowed in terms of national policy and has found it difficult to establish itself as something that is consistent and easily understood.

In this chapter we suggest that education policy and practice affecting 14–19-year-olds can best be analyzed using a two-dimensional historical and political framework (see Table 2.1). We have chosen to start our analysis in the mid-1980s with the introduction of the Technical and Vocational Education Initiative (TVEI) Extension, because this was the first time that the concept of a 14–19 curriculum[1] was placed in the public domain in England. This initiative was designed to offer a more applied curriculum with a particular stress on information technology, preparation for the workplace, recording of achievement and careers education for all young people between the ages of 14 and 18 (see Dale 1990 for details). We divide the 20 years that have elapsed since into four periods. While these can be distinguished from one another in several ways, we suggest that a driving influence has been shifts in the politics and ideology of the two major political parties while in government. These politically and ideologically defined periods provide the lenses through which policy-makers at the time sought to identify and address problems in the education and training system. However, politics and ideology, powerful though they are, provide only part of the explanation for the four phases of 14–19 policy we describe in this chapter. Four further shaping factors, listed on the vertical axis of Table 2.1, can be seen as historically important: participation, performance and labour market; curriculum, qualifications and assessment; organization and governance; and key debates.

PERIOD 1: MID-1980S AND THE SEMI-OFFICIAL CONCEPT OF 14–19

It was TVEI Extension in 1987[2] that first introduced the idea of 14–19 education into public discourse. However, the Department of Education and Science (DES), which was responsible for schools and the curriculum, had very little involvement in TVEI, which was an initiative sponsored by the Employment Department (ED), so education policy, institutions and qualifications were still largely framed in terms of the primary, secondary and 16–19 phases. The idea of 14–19 could, therefore, be seen as something 'semi-official' at this point – present but not dominant and very vulnerable

Table 2.1 A periodization of 14–19 policy from the mid-1980s to 2007

	Period 1. Mid-1980s Semi-official 14–19 concept	Period 2. Early 1990s Professional championship	Period 3. 1996–2001 16–19 under review 14–19 in abeyance	Period 4. 2001– 14-19 as official government policy
1. Politics and policy focus	Conservative pragmatic 'modernization' of the curriculum.	Conservative ideological phase – marketization and the development of a national triple-track qualifications system.	Period of review and pragmatic correction with a focus on 16–19 qualifications.	Education as part of New Labour's public service reform paradigm – diversity and choice.
2. Participation, performance and labour market	Growth in full-time post-16 participation and achievement due to GCSE; unregulated and active youth labour market.	Continued growth in full-time post-16 participation and achievement due to GCSE; youth labour market slows.	Plateauing of post-16 participation and slowing down of achievement, active youth labour market, particularly part-time.	Rises in full-time participation being offset by reduction in work-based route, achievement and retention rates rise significantly, less active youth labour market, concern about NEETs.
3. Curriculum, qualifications and assessment	TVEI Extension introduces 14–18 concept, curriculum innovation, introduction of GCSE, AS and modularization of A levels, vocationalization of the curriculum, core skills and NVQs.	Introduction of GNVQs as middle track, retrenchment of GCSEs and A levels, attempts to revive work-based route (e.g. Modern Apprenticeship). Proposals for diplomas.	Review of 16–19 qualifications (Capey 1995; Beaumont 1996; and Dearing 1996) leading to Curriculum 2000 reform process. More proposals for diplomas and overarching certification.	Relaxation of KS4, new 'vocational' alternatives for 14–16 year olds, Tomlinson reviews, 14–19 Diplomas, retrenchment of academic track, review and reform of Apprenticeship.
4. Organization and governance	Local collaboration through TVEI but beginnings of marketization (e.g. GM status for schools and CTCs); tertiary reorganization in some LEAs.	FE Incorporation and post-16 competition heightened by performance measures, TECs and training credits, central policy steering and declining role of LEAs.	Continued post-16 competition, specialist schools introduced but with strong direction from the centre and formation of the LSC.	14–19 collaboration v. institutional diversity and competition, LSC created but planning role short-lived and ceded to LAs. Moves towards greater devolution?
5. Key debates	*The New Vocationalism, breadth in advanced level learning, core skills, tertiary reorganization.*	*Marketization, international performance, unification and the academic/vocational divide, role of GNVQs/NVQs as a middle track.*	*Breadth in advanced level learning, standards v. inclusion, unification v. division, efficiency and effectiveness.*	*Unification v. division, manageability of the reform process, dilution of WBR, standards, devolution, planning v. markets.*

to policy changes, as the demise of TVEI in the early 1990s was to show.

The context for the emergence of 14–19 is the breakdown in the traditional relationship between the education and training system and the youth labour market. The growing issue of youth unemployment in the late 1970s led to a plethora of government-led initiatives (see, for example, Raggatt and Unwin 1991). The most important of these was the Youth Training Scheme. It aimed to delay entry to the youth labour market, which had been the traditional route for the majority of young people at 16 (Finegold and Soskice 1988).

The early 1980s witnessed a second wave of government interventions designed for 14–16-year-olds as well as for 16–19-year-olds. This eventually led to the launch of TVEI in 1983, which was initially piloted in schools and colleges in 14 local education authorities (LEAs) and designed for particular groups of learners in the middle or lower quartiles (Lord Young 1985, cited in Chitty 1991). Along with TVEI came new forms of post-16 pre-vocational and vocational certification for the 'new' sixth forms, for example Certificate of Pre-vocational Education (CPVE), and for the FE colleges (for example BEC and TEC) that were gradually developing into a distinct education sector (Mansell 1991).

According to Green (1991), it was two important reports – *Competence and Competition* (Institute of Manpower Studies 1984) and *A Challenge to Complacency* (Coopers and Lybrand 1985) – which adversely compared the UK record on training with that of other advanced industrial countries, that influenced government thinking about the role of education and training in economic performance. The most obvious outcome of this concern was the adoption of National Targets for Education and Training[3] in the early 1990s, but it also led to a third wave of government interventions, which although still designed to equip young people with the skills and knowledge required for employment were more educationally based. TVEI, for example, was extended to all 14–18-year-olds in the UK in 1987, taking a much broader focus. All learners were required to study technology, access work-related learning, develop the 'core competencies' required for further study and working life and to experience careers education and guidance (Taylor 1993). TVEI was thus seen by some commentators as a way of modernizing the secondary curriculum (for example Harland 1991) and even challenging the role of liberal education (Pring 1995). The curriculum processes promoted through TVEI (for example recording of achievement, careers education and guidance, work experience and core skills) could be interpreted as providing the beginnings of a core curriculum for the 14–19 phase and

TVEI's focus on progression between 14–16 and 16–19 education began to make the idea of a 14–19 phase more relevant.

As a result of TVEI, with its encouragement for schools and colleges to collaborate to provide a 14–19 entitlement and clear progression routes for learners, some LEAs, particularly those in areas with falling rolls, began to consider tertiary reorganization (for example Whitbread 1991). This development was seen by some commentators as a way of extending the comprehensive ideal to 16–19 education (for example Green 1991). However, at the same time, the 1988 Education Act allowed secondary schools to opt out of local authority control, thus making it more difficult for local authorities to create tertiary systems. In the post-16 sector, Training and Enterprise Councils (TECs) were announced in the White Paper *Employment for the 1990s* (DoE 1988) to create a market in training (Evans 1992).

By the end of the 1980s, therefore, two conflicting processes were taking shape. On the one hand, there was a tacit 'alliance' of forces willing to modernize education and training to make the curriculum more practical, vocational and flexible (Whiteside 1992). This alliance was seen to comprise the Employment Department with TVEI, the Confederation of British Industry (CBI) with its promotion of core skills, awarding bodies which were developing new forms of certification, education authorities with their tertiary reorganization proposals, various professional teacher organizations and many in the research community. On the other hand, however, was a more powerful set of political forces, including the DES, who were already pursuing a more ideological agenda that would come to fruition in the early 1990s. The Conservative 'pragmatic modernization' approach could thus be seen to be fading as the decade came to a close. The debates of the mid-1980s on vocationalism, core skills, breadth in advanced level learning and tertiary reorganization were not destined to influence mainstream Conservative policy on education in the early 1990s. Instead, they stimulated and supported a period of innovative 'bottom-up' developments led by local authorities and awarding bodies. These have been seen as a particular characteristic of the English system (Howieson et al. 1997), and have informed non-governmental reform proposals in the 1990s for a more unified and coherent 14–19 phase (Hodgson and Spours 1997a).

PERIOD 2: EARLY 1990S AND THE PROFESSIONAL CHAMPIONSHIP OF 14–19

The early 1990s could be seen as a period of retreat for the 14–19 concept. Bottom-up initiatives, which had flourished during the 1980s, were replaced by top-down national reform (Richardson et al. 1993). TVEI faded as its funding ceased and schools focused on the introduction of the subject-based National Curriculum, restricting space for the vocationalization of the curriculum (Cockett 1996). At this point, post-16 qualifications became the focus of reform for government and for other organizations and political parties (for example Finegold et al. 1990; Labour Party 1992; NCE 1995). The idea of 14–19 as a curriculum and qualifications concept was kept alive by a number of education professional organizations outside the Government (for example SHA 1994; Crombie-White et al. 1995). The National Association of Headteachers had led the way in 1987 with the publication of *Action Plan: A Policy 14–18* (NAHT 1987) and by the mid-1990s, the idea of 14–19 and a more unified qualifications system began to replace the separate debates about 16–19 and 14–19 (for example NUT 1995; Labour Party 1996).

These radical proposals were, however, taking place against the backcloth of the Conservative's restructuring of the education state, which had started in the late 1980s with the 1988 Education Reform Act and which gathered pace in the early 1990s. The main features of this new public management paradigm (Newman 2000) were more central control through arms' length bodies, such the Further Education Funding Council (FEFC) and the National Council for Vocational Qualifications (NCVQ), and the attempted creation of a market in education and training through institutional competition.

The early 1990s was also a significant period for qualifications development with the creation of new national triple-track post-16 system comprising A Levels for the most able, GNVQs for those in the middle quartiles and NVQs for those wanting occupationally specific or work-based qualifications (Hodgson and Spours 1997a). A subordinate but, nevertheless, significant proposal was for the introduction of Ordinary and Advanced Diplomas in 1994 to coincide with the first award of GNVQs. The main aim of these Diplomas was to encourage learners to participate by recognizing the equivalence of GNVQs and NVQs to A Levels, although they could also be seen as a weak response to the IPPR proposals for *A British Baccalaureate* (Finegold et al. 1990) which had gathered widespread media and professional support in the period prior to the publication of the White Paper.

In the event, the diploma proposals quietly disappeared as the Conservatives focused their attention on the triple-track system. They concentrated on making the academic track more 'restrictive' by a series of related measures – reducing the role of internal assessment in GCSEs and

A Levels, suppressing innovative modular A Level experiments such as the Wessex Project, introducing tiered GCSE papers and an A* grade and emphasizing the distinction between 'good GCSEs' (that is A*–C grades) and passes at the lower grades through the introduction of performance tables (Richardson et al. 1993). In order to preserve the more selective academic track while responding to rising participation rates, GNVQs were designed to be offered in schools as well as colleges and to lead to the workplace and higher education.

The idea of a 14–19 phase or even a common 14–19 entitlement simply faded from policy along with TVEI. Even the development of core skills, later to be known as key skills, which had been seen by the Government in the late 1980s as a potential part of all 16–19 learner programmes, was halted in 1991 due to political concerns about standards within A Levels (Richardson 1993). Core skills were then developed solely within broad vocational programmes, such as GNVQs, which became the Conservative Government's main response to rising post-16 participation rates and the vehicle through which much of the curriculum innovation of the late 1980s would be channelled (Higham et al. 1996). Similarly, collaboration between schools and colleges to aid progression from pre-16 to post-16 education, which TVEI had begun to foster, was swept aside by the institutional competition that accompanied the marketization of post-16 education and training instigated by the 1992 *Further and Higher Education Act* (Green and Lucas 1999).

Key debates related to the education and training of 14–19 year olds during this period not only focused on these new institutional arrangements and the effects of marketization more broadly (for example Bates and Riseborough 1993; Hodkinson 1996), but also included concerns about the performance of post-16 education and training, particularly when compared internationally (for example Ryan 1992), about the reinforcement of the academic/vocational divide (for example Richardson et al. 1993; Hodgson and Spours 1997b) and the role of the new national vocational qualifications, GNVQs and NVQs (for example Hyland 1994; Smithers 1994). The early 1990s were characterized by frentic politically and ideologically driven education and training reform which, by the middle of the decade, was beginning to experience significant problems. Even before the election of New Labour in 1997, the education policy of the Conservative Government, now under a new Secretary of State, Gillian Shephard, began to move in a more pragmatic direction. Thus began a period of reviews that survived the handover of political power from a Conservative to a New Labour Administration.

PERIOD 3: 16–19 UNDER REVIEW AND 14–19 IN ABEYANCE (1996–2001)

In 1996, the concept of 14–19 made a surprise return to the national stage for a brief moment with the publication of the White Paper *Learning to Compete: Education and Training for 14–19 Year Olds* (DfEE 1996). This document was a response to problems arising from the triple-track qualifications system. Its central proposals were to introduce a range of vocational alternatives for pre-16 learners, to develop National Traineeships for 16–19-year-olds to replace Youth Training and to provide a learning credit entitlement for all 14–19-year-olds. However, while *Learning to Compete* purported to promote a 14–19 perspective, it was not a strongly 14–19 document. Most of it was devoted to 16–19 education and training and constituted the Conservative Government's response to the Capey Review of GNVQs (1995), the Beaumont Review of NVQs and Scottish Vocational Qualifications (1996), the consultation on the funding of Youth Training and Modern Apprenticeships and the more comprehensive Dearing *Review of Qualifications for 16–19 Year Olds* (Dearing 1996).

The plans outlined in this White Paper were not, in fact, implemented by a Conservative Government. Instead, the proposals on 16–19 qualifications appeared in the new Secretary of State, David Blunkett's, consultation document, *Qualifying for Success* (DfEE/DENI/WO 1997), as the new Labour Government attempted to put its own imprimatur on proposals borrowed directly from the Dearing Review. The concept of a 14–19 curriculum was, once again, forgotten. *Aiming Higher: Labour's Proposal for the Reform of the 14–19+ Curriculum* (Labour Party 1996) was ignored. Instead, the incoming government's focus moved to qualifications for 16–19-year-olds as it pursued its Manifesto commitments to 'support broader A Levels, up-grade vocational qualifications underpinned by rigorous standards and key skills' (Labour Party 1997).

The scene was set for what became known as *Curriculum 2000* and a period of consultation and implementation of what could be regarded as Conservative policy on advanced level qualifications. *Qualifying for Success* proposed to:

- break A Levels into two three-unit blocks, AS and A2, which together formed an A Level;
- introduce a new Advanced Extension Award (AEA) to stretch those working at the top end of A Levels;
- make changes to GNVQs to align them more with A Levels in terms of grading and structure;

- introduce a Key Skills Qualification in Communication, Application of Number and IT; and
- 'to work in the longer term towards an overarching certificate, building on the Dearing proposals for National Certificates and a National Advanced Diploma' (DfEE/DENI/WO 1997: 23).

Apart from *Qualifying for Success*, which led to *Curriculum 2000*, the other main qualifications reform was the enlargement and rationalization of the National Qualifications Framework to include a wider range of qualifications than previously and to better secure their public recognition.

New Labour's vision for this period was to take a path between the radical unifying proposals, which had influenced the Labour Party in opposition and led to *Aiming Higher*, and the focus on A Level distinctiveness promoted by Dearing. While the Government broadly implemented the Dearing proposals, the emphasis was on broadening the advanced level curriculum, creating greater access to A Levels and forming 'linkages' between the three qualification tracks (Raffe et al. 1998). There was even a short flirtation with overarching certification as Baroness Blackstone commissioned research into its feasibility (QCA, CCEA and ACCAC 1998). However, during this period, preparation for and the implementation of *Curriculum 2000* preoccupied both policy-makers and practitioners and the 14–19 concept, as well as an overarching certificate, were quietly put on the backburner.

Attention quickly switched to problems of governance and organization when a review of the TECs and concerns about the mismanagement of post-16 funding led to the publication of *Learning to Succeed* (DfEE 1999). This document proposed the formation of the Learning and Skills Council (LSC), from a merger of the TECs and FEFC, to be responsible for funding and planning all post-16 education and training outside higher education. This reform, together with the formation of the Qualifications and Curriculum Authority (QCA) and the rationalization of awarding bodies, suggested that the reforming zeal of New Labour was being channelled into streamlining the Conservative education state to ensure stronger central control of policy and delivery.

The major debates during this period continued to be about the effects of marketization and the fact that New Labour was not contesting what was a Conservative political paradigm (for example Ball et al. 2000; Whitty 2002) and the effectiveness of New Labour's social inclusion agenda (for example Pearce and Hilman 1998). More directly connected with 14–19 were debates on breadth in advanced level learning (for example AoC et al.

1997; Pound 1999), standards versus inclusion (for example Hodgson and Spours 2003), unification versus division (for example Raffe et al. 1998) and the inefficiency and inequity of the funding system (DfEE 1999). However, these debates were not influential as the Government doggedly pursued its Manifesto commitments.

PERIOD 4: 14–19 AS OFFICIAL GOVERNMENT POLICY (2001 – PRESENT)

The 14–19 Green Paper (2002)

In 2002, the New Labour Government announced a 'new 14-19 phase' (Morris 2002: 3) some 15 years after its first appearance in public discourse. While the Labour Party in Opposition had discussed plans for the reform of the 14-19+ curriculum (Labour Party 1996), in government the focus in the first Parliament was firmly on getting 'the basics right in primary schools' (Morris 2002: 3). It was only in 2001 in *Schools Achieving Success* (DfES 2001a) that Estelle Morris, Secretary of State for Education, laid out her plans for modernization of the secondary curriculum and promised to publish a consultation document designed to create 'a more coherent 14-19 phase of education, including improved vocational education and greater flexibility after 14' (DfES 2001b). This White Paper also announced the Increased Flexibility Programme (IFP) that funded colleges to work with schools on offering work-related learning for 14-16-year-olds.

The promised consultation document, entitled *14-19 Education: Extending Opportunities, Raising Standards* (DfES 2002), was published in February of the following year. Its main proposals were:

• to reduce the level of prescription at Key Stage 4;
• to offer more opportunities for vocational learning;
• an entitlement to a Modern Apprenticeship place for all 16-17-year-olds with five GCSE passes including English and maths; and
• a 'matriculation diploma' at Intermediate, Advanced and Higher levels.

An important sub-theme of the 14-19 Green Paper was to 'allow young people to develop at a pace consistent with their abilities' (DfES 2002: 46) with the emphasis on 'acceleration' in which GCSEs would become less like a school-leaving examination and more like a 'progress check' (2002: 21) as part of a more coherent 14-19 phase. In an attempt to offset emerging criticisms of standards in *Curriculum 2000*, the Government proposed a new Distinction grade for A Levels. Alongside these curricular reforms, the Green Paper attempted to support 14-19 institutional arrangements and collaboration through new 14–19, rather than 16–19, area-wide inspections.

New Labour's delayed recognition of the importance of the 14–19 phase could be seen as the result of what has been termed 'policy sequence' (Hodgson and Spours 1999). In its first five years, the Government concerned itself mainly with nursery and primary education, only to move later to the secondary phase, Key Stage 3 and 14–19 education and training as a whole. This new focus was explained as a way of building on the successes of earlier phases of reform and to improve the breadth outcomes of *Curriculum 2000*, which was recognized as having experienced 'difficulties' in its first year of implementation (DfES 2002: 33). This approach to reform, in which the Government pursued its own education 'policy hierarchies', had the effect of producing 14–19 proposals, which did not connect or substantially draw on the 14–19 debates of the 1990s instigated by the education profession and policy think tanks.

While representatives of the education profession broadly welcomed the focus on 14–19 and flexibility in Key Stage 4, many of the Green Paper proposals were given short shrift. Practitioner professional associations criticized what they saw as its utilitarian vision, proposals for learning acceleration, the Distinction A Level grade and the matriculation diploma model (for example AoC 2002; ATL 2002). These organizations, along with many others who responded to the consultation (there were almost 2,000 written responses), felt that more radical reform affecting GCSEs and A Levels, as well as vocational awards, was required and that the matriculation diplomas were 'weak wrappers' around existing inadequate qualifications.

The demands for a more radical approach to 14–19 reform were also shaped by two other factors. The first was the so-called A Level grading crisis in the summer of 2002 in which an awarding body was accused of manipulating grades in order to depress pass rates in the new A Levels (Richardson 2007) (see Chapter 3 for more details). This crisis shook confidence in *Curriculum 2000* and, more importantly in the 'A level gold-standard', thus opening a window for more far-reaching reforms to be considered. The second was the appointment of a new Minister, David Miliband, who was able to consider a fresh approach to 14–19 reform. As a co-author of IPPR's *A British Baccalaureate* in 1990, his willingness to see the potential of a unified qualifications framework put him more in touch with professional opinion than his predecessors.

The Government's response (2003)

The Government's response to the consultation on the Green Paper was

14–19 Excellence and Opportunity (DfES 2003) which, amongst proposals for increasing flexibility in Key Stage 4, also established a working group under the chairmanship of an ex Chief HMI, Mike Tomlinson, to examine longer-term 14–19 reform. While many of the short-term changes outlined in the original Green Paper, with the notable exception of the Matriculation Diplomas, were accepted, the thinking and tone of *14–19 Excellence and Opportunity* were very different from the earlier consultation document. It sounded a note of urgency in terms of education and training system per-formance by focusing on the 17+ participation figure and the fact that the UK was equal 25th out of 29 OECD countries, just ahead of Greece, Mexico and Turkey.

More importantly, and something that was to shape events over the next two years, was its comments on GCSEs and A Levels. Out of the 10 criticisms of the current education system, no less than seven of them related directly to these qualifications. In previous government documents in this area, it was vocational qualifications and the work-based route that were normally singled out for comment. In *14–19 Excellence and Opportunity*, however, the GCSE was seen as contributing to truanting and poor behaviour in the last two years of compulsory education and it was even suggested that young people were 'bored by their GCSE studies' (DfES 2003: 10). It was now viewed as a barrier to participation for those young people who saw themselves as 'failures' because they did not achieve five A*–C grades. A Levels, despite the *Curriculum 2000* reforms, were described as providing narrow programmes of study. Moreover, there were concerns about the amount of assessment and the lack of challenge for the most able. Vocational awards were characterized as 'a jungle of alternative courses and qualifications, too many of which lack status, clarity of purpose and brand recognition with employers' (2003: 11) and Modern Apprenticeships were dubbed 'variable' in quality with 'unacceptably low completion rates' (2003: 11). This picture of 14–19 education and training in England was then contrasted unfavourably with other national systems. These were seen to perform more effectively as a result of five key features: a common curriculum in the lower secondary phase; continuation of a broad range of subjects in the upper secondary phase; vocational routes providing access to higher education; measures to engage disaffected students; and grouped awards, like the French Baccalaureate (DfES 2003: 12).

The 14–19 White Paper concluded with a remit for an independent working group to consider three strategic directions for change: coherence in 14–19 learning programmes for all young people; making assessment arrangements more appropriate and manageable; and developing a unified framework of qualifications. The scene was set for two years of unprecedented discussion about a new long-term vision for 14–19 education and training.

The Tomlinson Working Group (2003–2004)

Throughout the latter half of 2003 until October 2004, 14–19 education and training became a high-profile topic of public debate for the first time in England, involving large numbers of policy-makers and researchers and thousands of education professionals in an extensive consultation exercise. Mike Tomlinson's Working Group of 14 individuals, selected for their expertise in either research, policy, business acumen or education practice, was supported by three sub-groups tasked with examining assessment, coherent learner programmes and a unified qualifications framework, six stakeholder groups focusing, for example, on young people, employers and higher education, and two technical groups. Consultation events were held across the country and the main Working Group and the task groups met very regularly and were expected to explain and receive feedback on current thinking at professional conferences and seminars.

Proposals for a unified diploma system

As a result of their work, three reports were published. The first (Working Group on 14–19 Reform 2003a) set out the principles for reform and the main approach to planning, assessment and qualifications. Its summary document (Working Group on 14–19 Reform 2003b) stressed the need for all 14–19-year-olds to have 'a balanced curriculum' comprising three types of learning: 'the general skills and knowledge which everybody needs for adult life and to undertake further learning and employment'; 'specialized learning, such as specific academic or vocational knowledge and skills which enable them to progress to the higher education, training or career path which they want to follow'; and 'supplementary learning which will help support their progress' (2003b: 4). More controversially, the Tomlinson first report proposed 'a new diploma framework' for all 14–19-year-olds, 'covering the whole of their learning programme, rather than existing individual qualifications such as GCSEs, GNVQs, A Levels and NVQs' (2003b: 4). Moreover, it was suggested that young people would 'take fewer written examinations than now; and assessment by their teachers, lecturers and trainers would be given more importance' (2003b: 5).

These radical proposals for a new diploma system that would gradually subsume all existing qualifications for 14–19-year-olds from Entry to Advanced Level, and with less external assessment, were widely consulted upon and formed the basis of the diploma designs laid out in some detail in the Interim Report in February 2004 (Working Group on 14–19 Reform 2004b).

Five key debates

While everyone within the Working Group and sub-groups supported the radical analysis contained within *14–19: Opportunity and Excellence*, there were sharp debates in a number of areas central to the remit from ministers.[4] The first was about the role of *Curriculum 2000* and whether wholesale reform of A Levels was, indeed, required. Some in the Working Group argued that the reforms had achieved a degree of breadth for advanced level students, while others judged *Curriculum 2000* to have largely failed and suggested that a more radical diploma framework was needed.

A second related issue was how a diploma system would distinguish between high performers in terms of grading of A Level components, something which universities were keen to see in any new system. Not everyone in the Working Group saw this as a major priority, because the proposed Advanced Diploma was seen as very demanding. However, in the event, a strategic compromise was reached. Committee members agreed to the introduction of A+ and A++ grades for some advanced level components, providing that the diploma system as a whole was fully inclusive from Entry Level upwards. This balance could be summarized in the phrase 'open at the bottom and tough at the top'.

A third area of debate concerned the balance between flexibility and coherence in learner programmes, with those representing the FE sector in particular arguing for a loose credit-based framework and others supporting a more baccalaureate-type award. Again, a compromise was struck, but the balance tipped more towards coherence than credit-based flexibility, making the proposed diploma framework different from the Scottish modular system. The fourth debate was about how much vocational specialization was appropriate for 14–16-year-olds. The Working Group recognized the motivational value of sharply vocational experiences in the last two years of compulsory education but stressed the importance of keeping options open until 16. The result was that only an 'open diploma' was available pre-16, after which 'named' and more specialized diplomas in both vocational and general education could be achieved.

Finally, there was a discussion about the relationship between apprenticeships and the proposed diploma system. A submission to the Working

Group suggested that diplomas should lead to apprenticeships and thus would not be part of the new diploma framework. This was rejected and the final report stressed that apprenticeships should be integrated within the diploma system itself, thus increasing its reach and inclusivity.

The response to the Final Report

In October 2004, the Working Group published its Final Report (Working Group on 14-19 Reform 2004a). Over the period of the three reports, a broad consensus for reform had been built. The nature of this process was summed up by one of our interviewees:

> *What we wanted to see was a consensus emerging, which in the end Mike Tomlinson managed to produce, around what was needed to be done. And we've always recognized that this wasn't something that could be introduced by a wave of the wand of a government minister. It had to be something that was acceptable to employers, that was acceptable to universities, and specifically the Russell Group universities, and to the schools and colleges who were going to be delivering the qualifications. (PA 19)*

Early on there were dissenting voices in the media, primarily expressing concern about the loss of A Levels (for example *Daily Mail* 2004; Smithers 2004), the speed of reform and the possibility of extra work for teachers because of increased internal assessment (for example Townsend 2004). For the most part, however, there was considerable professional excitement about the possibility of holistic rather than piecemeal reform (for example Stanistreet 2004; Flint 2004) and even those newspapers not normally supportive of the Government were cautiously positive (for example Clare 2004; *Financial Times* 2004).

Educational professionals, who had championed the cause of a more unified and inclusive 14-19 phase throughout the 1990s, saw this as the point where their ideas were finally being taken seriously and might shape the future 14-19 system:

> *So you could argue very, very strongly that the degree of embeddedness, of commitment to Tomlinson reforms, wasn't a flash in the pan, it was actually a nexus of the debates that we'd been having for years ... actually, what Tomlinson did was not so much by dint of heroic leadership to secure a consensus, but what he was doing was gathering together a whole set of ideas that were very prevalent at the time and pulling them together in a coherent form. (PA 11)*

With education ministers making supportive noises, all stakeholder groups having been consulted and the A Level brand, for so long the sticking point for radical change, having been tarnished as a result of the 'crises' in the summer of 2002, the scene was set for a positive government response to the efforts of the Working Group on 14–19 Reform.

The Government rejects the Tomlinson proposals

However, this is not quite what happened because as Mike Tomlinson was 'beavering away, the political landscape was changing' (Baker 2005). According to Mike Baker, the BBC's education correspondent, the opportunities for radical reform rapidly diminished as Tomlinson's recommendations sailed into the choppy waters of a pre-election period, with the Tories expected to back the retention of GCSEs and A Levels (Curtis 2004). While education ministers lauded the Final Report when it was launched on 18 October and was being warmly received by the media (for example BBC News 2004a), the very same night the Prime Minister, Tony Blair, in a speech to the CBI stated 'GCSEs and A Levels will stay. So will externally marked exams' (Blair 2004). There was no mention in his speech of the Diploma system. Instead, Blair misrepresented the Tomlinson Report as 'establishing a number of clearly defined vocational pathways to be available from the age of 14.' His speech thus signalled that the main Tomlinson proposals were unlikely to be accepted by the Government.

The Government's retreat from radical reform was reinforced by changes to the education ministerial team, which had overseen and supported the Tomlinson Working Group. In December 2004, following David Blunkett's resignation from the Home Office, Charles Clarke (the Secretary of State for Education) was asked to replace him and David Miliband was moved to the Cabinet Office to lead the writing of Labour's Election Manifesto. They were replaced by Ruth Kelly, as Secretary of State for Education, who was totally new to education and to a ministerial position. Andrew Adonis, previously head of the Downing Street Policy Unit and a supporter of A Levels, was also brought in as Schools Minister. The death knell of Tomlinson had been sounded.

Reflections on the Final Report

With the benefit of hindsight, the Final Report of the Working Group faced several problems. The most obvious, and the one which was voiced repeatedly in 2005 following the publication of the Government's 14–19 White Paper response to Tomlinson, was that political expediency had triumphed over education logic (Dunford 2005). Given the totemic status of A Levels, it was unlikely that any minister would want to be known as the person who abolished these publicly recognized exams (even though their 'abolition' was not, in fact, advocated in the Tomlinson Report). But there were other reasons why the Final Report would have faced difficulties, even if a general election had not been pending. The proposals of the Working Group were seen as simply too complex. Jeremy Paxman, when interviewing Mike Tomlinson on the day of the Interim Report's publication, stated 'I can't understand a lot of it' (BBC News 2004b). This complexity arose not only from a system-wide approach to reform, but also from a desire to forge a consensus across a broad political and professional range of opinion. While the Working Group had deliberated for 18 months, historically speaking this was a very short period for the huge task it had been given and to shift wider public opinion. The painful fact was that the unification debates of the 1990s had only reached the education profession and some national agencies, but had not permeated into the public psyche.

While in retrospect there can be self-criticism, the disappointment and frustration felt because of the Government's rejection of the main proposals and spirit of Tomlinson still lingers (*Independent* 2007). As one interviewee commented, 'the rejection of Tomlinson destroyed what was really quite a fragile unity ... and it created a very bad climate because we just thought "well what's that all been about then" ' (PA 18).

The 14–19 White Paper and beyond

In February 2005, Ruth Kelly published the Government's official response to the Tomlinson Final Report. The White Paper *14–19 Education and Skills* (DfES 2005a) rejected the main Tomlinson recommendation for a unified multi-level diploma system. Instead, it proposed the development of 14 lines of 'Specialised Diplomas' (see Chapter 4) to provide a ladder of progression of broad vocational qualifications throughout the 14–19 phase, together with modifications to GCSE and A Level specifications (see Chapter 3). These new qualifications formed the centre-piece of the first ever statutory 14–19 National Entitlement for learners, aimed at providing both breadth and choice of study and institutional setting (see Chapter 1 for detail). As part of its focus on vocational education, the Government promised to expand the apprenticeships system and to introduce a vocationally orientated pilot programme to engage disaffected 14–16-year-olds (see Chapter 5).

The White Paper's analysis of the problems facing the 14–19 phase was very different from that of both the Tomlinson reports and the Government's own previous document *14–19: Opportunity and Excellence*. Its perspective on the weaknesses of the English system was almost identical to that of the 2002 14–19 Green Paper. It saw the problem, once again, in terms of basic skills and weak vocational provision. On the other hand, A Levels and GCSEs were viewed as 'by far the most well recognized and understood route to success' (DfES 2005a: 19) and would be retained 'as cornerstones of the new system' (2005a: 6). What followed this analysis was a 'cherry-picking' of the Tomlinson proposals. Its broad unified diploma template was applied to the new vocational Diplomas that would co-exist with GCSEs and A Levels. As we will see in Chapter 4, this position would mean that Diplomas would become alternatives to A Levels rather than the basis for the 14–19 system as a whole. Moreover, the Tomlinson principle of inclusivity would be further compromised. The Diplomas in the White Paper were confined to Levels 1–3, leaving Entry Level adrift. The Government had to compensate for this later by announcing a Foundation Learning Tier (see Chapter 3). Finally, the Tomlinson proposals for more internal professional-led assessment were restricted to Key Stage 3, leaving 14–19 qualifications still largely driven by external examinations. What would be seen as a divided approach to qualifications reform would be ameliorated by a stress on institutional collaboration to support the new 14–19 Entitlement (see Chapter 6).

In October 2007, however, Ed Balls, the new Secretary of State at the Department for Children, Schools and Families (DCSF), announced the introduction of three new lines of Diplomas in science, languages and humanities. This was shortly followed by his declaration that the age of participation would be raised to 17 in 2013 and 18 in 2015. Several of our interviewees commented on what they saw as a new climate in policy-making. The announcement of the three new Diplomas was seen as a 'step in the right direction' (PA 19) and a 'huge cultural shift ... because it has broken the link between diplomas being associated with sectors' (PA 14). Some even described it as a 'big, big step forward ... because it starts to give you more of what Tomlinson envisaged as an overarching diploma, where everything is fitted in' (PA 22). In most interviewees' minds, the perceived change in policy had resulted from what one described as 'a shift in political personnel and political beliefs' (PA 5).

The question we pose in different chapters in the book is whether these developments mark a shift in government policy towards a more unified and universal upper secondary phase in England or simply a pragmatic adjustment to a divided system.

CONCLUSION: PARTIAL APPROACHES AND RECYCLED POLICY SOLUTIONS

As we have seen, the idea of a 14–19 phase of education and training has been part of policy-maker and practitioner discourse since the mid-1980s. Over this period, it has waxed and waned in terms of national policy priorities and has only become a prominent policy feature since 2002. Moreover, the development of a 14–19 phase has been marked by policy vacillation and partial reform, allowing historical weaknesses of the English education and training system to persist: selective general education, remedial approaches to further and vocational education, a weak work-based route and complex and fragmented institutional delivery arrangements. It could be argued, therefore, that despite the present Labour Government's avowed commitment to 14–19 learning, policy in this area has largely continued what began as a Conservative initiative. Meanwhile, the main organizational and qualifications landscape, despite all the rhetoric and turbulence, remains largely unchanged. Amidst the different periods of 14–19 reform in England, one feature stands out – the association of the 14–19 concept with the provision of a vocational alternative route and thus with a divided system.

The Government hopes that its emphasis on building a clear vocational route as an alternative to GCSEs and A Levels will address historic weaknesses in the English system. Historical analysis, on the other hand, suggests that a continued focus on an 'alternative' full-time vocational route demonstrates a lack of policy learning, with a recycling of the policy mistakes of the past (Higham and Yeomans 2007a). 14–19 reform is yet again associated with low-status learners and certain institutions, rather than with the whole cohort and all providers. This allows the most selective schools and their learners to ignore the reform process, with significant implications for the public recognition of both 14–19 reform and the very concept of a 14–19 phase itself. The problem of reform, therefore, is not simply about policy but also about how policy impacts on potentially change-resistant institutions (see Chapter 6 on organization and governance).

The idea of a comprehensive and more unified phase still remains subordinate, despite its steady intellectual march in the 1990s and its temporary flowering under David Miliband and Mike Tomlinson. It is hard not to conclude that, regardless of phases of policy development, the period from the mid-1980s to the present broadly constitutes a single 'political era' (Hodgson and Spours 2006b), which has left us with a divided 14–19 phase.

NOTES

[1] In fact, TVEI was often also described in terms of 14–18-year-olds, but the concept of a phase that linked the last two years of compulsory education with the initial years of post-compulsory education is the same whether it is described as 14–18 or 14–19. For the purposes of this book we will use the term 14–19.

[2] TVEI was first introduced in 1983 but was a pilot in only a small number of LEAs at this point, so we begin our history in 1987 when the concept of 14–19 became much more public as a result of TVEI being extended to all LEAs.

[3] The National Targets for Education and Training (NTETs) set out in 1990 were for 85 per cent of young people to achieve Level 2 by the age of 19, 75 per cent to achieve a Level 2 in the key skills of communications, IT and Numeracy by the age of 19 and 60 per cent to achieve Level 3 by age 21 by the year 2000 (NACETT 1994).

[4] Minutes and internal documents of the Working Group are not in the public domain. The discussion which follows draws on the authors' personal experiences as members of this review.

chapter 3

REFORMING GENERAL EDUCATION

GCSES, A LEVELS AND THE ISSUE OF STANDARDS

General Certificates of Secondary Education (GCSEs) and A Levels, which largely represent the general education track in England and dominate the 14–19 curriculum as a whole, are widely recognized by the general public. Yet every year in August, the media raises concerns about declining standards and there is a rehearsal of a bizarre English ritual. Employers' complain about young people's lack of basic skills at 16+. Universities lament 18-year-olds' inability to construct extended pieces of writing and bemoan the difficulties of selecting the 'most able' young people for prestigious courses. As part of its 14–19 reform agenda, the Government has tried to address the situation by retaining the GCSE and A Level brand on the one hand, while adjusting the qualifications internally to tackle some of the criticisms levelled at the two awards on the other hand.

This chapter considers the English approach to general education within an international perspective. It identifies its main features and provides a short history of its development in England over the last couple of decades as the context for a discussion of current trends in GCSEs and A levels. The latter part of the chapter is devoted to a description of the changes the Government will introduce to this area in September 2008. We conclude by suggesting that these reforms can be viewed in four different ways, depending on the observer. From an international perspective, the latest developments do not constitute a fundamental change to the English approach to upper secondary general education. Looked at through a national historical lens, the reforms in this area appear to constitute the latest wave of retrenchment in a long history of policies to open up and then close down access to the general education track. However, from a practitioner viewpoint, the changes to GCSEs and A Levels, the introduction of functional skills qualifications, the Foundation Learning Tier, the Extended Project (and, in some cases the International Baccalaureate, the 'Pre-U' qualification and iGCSEs) all signal a period of considerable turbulence (yet again). These require new approaches to pedagogy, to the organization of learning and teaching, and to advice and guidance for young people. For learners, the reforms will have differentiated effects, with those at the top of the ability range arguably benefiting most.

14–19 GENERAL EDUCATION IN ENGLAND THROUGH AN INTERNATIONAL LENS

Despite the existence of a national curriculum for compulsory schooling to the age of 16, general education for 14–19-year-olds in England is primarily defined by two national examinations that young people take at the ages of 15/16 and 17/18 – GCSEs and A levels. Since 2002, the National Curriculum ensures that all 14–16-year-olds follow a course of study in English, mathematics, science, ICT, physical education, citizenship, work-related learning and enterprise, religious education and health and careers education.[1] At the age of 16, the vast majority of young people in England, Wales and Northern Ireland sit one or more GCSEs, with most taking at least five and a significant minority taking 10 or more (JCQ 2007a).[2] The most common options are science, mathematics, English, English literature and design and technology (JCQ 2007b). GCSE passes are graded from A*–G, with five A*–C grades commonly seen as a passport to advanced study and now often described by government agencies as 'a full Level 2' or an 'Intermediate award' (LSC 2005). This benchmark, which is the focus of school accountability, is also the most widely cited in the media when judging both individual learner and institutional performance at 16+ (Stobart 2008).

While it is possible to leave the education system at the age of 16, in 2006 77 per cent[3] of young people in England remained in some form of education and training between the ages of 16–18, with 61 per cent on full-time courses (DfES 2007a). Of these full-time learners about two-thirds (40 per cent of the total cohort) took advanced level qualifications, with three-quarters of this group on A Level traditional and applied programmes (that is the Advanced Certificate of Vocational Education),[4] demonstrating the continuing dominance of this qualification in the English system. The remainder of the cohort is either on full-time courses leading to general or vocational qualifications at Intermediate, Foundation or Entry Level or on work-based learning programmes (just under 7 per cent of the cohort) – see Chapters 4 and 5 for more detail.

Learners can decide which subjects they wish to study at A Level. Since the inception of *Curriculum 2000*, which introduced a two-stage Advanced Subsidiary (AS)/A2 approach to A Levels,[5] most learners take four subjects at AS Level in the first year of post-compulsory study and continue on to three full A Levels in their second year (Hodgson and Spours 2003). In 2007 in the UK as a whole, the six most popular subjects at both AS and A Level were English, mathematics, general studies, biology, psychology and history (JCQ 2007c) – none of these is considered an 'Applied' subject. In 2007 across the UK, the entries for Applied AS awards (50,982) and for Applied A Levels (15,556) were tiny in comparison with those for AS Levels (1,114,424) and A Levels (805,657) (JCQ 2007d).

16–19-year-olds not only have a choice over what qualifications they wish to take (assuming they have the required prior attainment), but also where they want to study. In 2006, about half of 16–18-year-olds in full-time education in England were studying in further education or sixth form colleges, with the rest in school sixth forms, either maintained (31 per cent) or independent (7 per cent), or in higher education institutions (13 per cent) (DfES 2007a) – see Chapter 6 for more detail.

From these basic facts and figures, looking at the English 14–19 general education system through an international lens, it is possible to identify nine defining features (see Figure 3.1).

---

1 Qualifications-led
2 Dominated by GCSEs and A Levels
3 Selective at 16+
4 Accredited and influenced by privatized examination and awarding bodies
5 'Elective' with considerable learner choice in terms of programmes of study post-16
6 Individual subject and qualification focused rather than programmatic
7 Minimal focus on entitlement
8 Little curriculum breadth – particularly post-16
9 School- and-college based

Figure 3.1 *Defining features of the English 14–19 general education system*

First and foremost, the system can be characterized as qualifications-led, dominated by GCSEs and A Levels, and overwhelmingly education-based.

The role of the examination and awarding bodies in such a qualifications-dominated system is thus crucial. The fact that there are several of these bodies, that they are private organizations (for the most part with charitable status) competing for business, and that they are overseen by an arms-length regulatory body – the Qualifications and Curriculum Authority (QCA) – rather than an education ministry is something that never ceases to amaze observers from other countries studying the English education system.[6] Moreover, qualifications are largely seen as a tool for selection rather than for progression. It is not normally possible, for example, for a young person to remain in general education after the age of 16 unless he or she gains the equivalent of five GCSEs at grades A*–C. At this point, those not achieving this benchmark are usually only offered vocational or work-based options.

For most young people education is relatively broad in terms of the number of subjects studied up until the age of 16. However, compulsory breadth for 14–16-year-olds has been considerably reduced since the National Curriculum was originally introduced. It is now narrow in comparison with many Western European countries, causing concern among educationalists and more widely about the loss of arts, humanities and modern foreign languages as part of all young people's education at this point (Hayward et al. 2006). Post-16 programmes of study are choice-based and specialist, with the majority of learners studying three or fewer subjects with little or no concept of a holistic programme of learning. Again, in comparison with general education programmes in other European education systems, this is considerably narrower in curricular terms and more individual-subject focused. The limited and voluntary measures brought in as part of the *Curriculum 2000* reforms – the possibility of taking four or five AS Levels in the first year of study; the opportunity to mix more applied and more theoretical qualifications; the Advanced Extension Award (AEA) to provide 'stretch and challenge' for the most able learners; the introduction of new so-called 'broadening' AS Levels, such as critical thinking and a Key Skills AS qualification in communications, application of number and IT – simply did not succeed in broadening the advanced level curriculum. Three A Levels remained the most common outcome for learners in the general education track (see Hodgson and Spours 2003). Finally, GCSEs and, more particularly, A Levels – the so-called 'gold standard' – have been a politically sensitive area of education policy for at least the last 20 years (Hodgson and Spours 1999) and continue to be so (Raffe and Spours 2007).

This combination of features marks the English general education system out from the majority of its international counterparts – a point which was recognized by both the Dearing Review of 16–19 Qualifications (Dearing 1996) and the more recent final report of the Tomlinson Working Group on 14–19 Reform (2004a), but has yet to be addressed by education policy. In fact, as we discuss below, the issue of curriculum breadth in general education, which formed part of policy deliberations earlier in the New Labour Administration, now appears to have been buried. Instead, the Government has been focusing its attention on the Diplomas and on tinkering with the design of GCSEs and A Levels in an attempt to head off further criticism of these qualifications.

GENERAL EDUCATION IN ENGLAND: A BRIEF HISTORY

A Levels have been the major shaping factor in general education in England for more than 60 years. Previously O Levels and, since 1986, GCSEs have functioned not only as broad general education but also as sifts for the so-called 'royal route' via A Levels to higher education. However, the nature of A Level domination has changed over the years. When they were introduced in 1950, they were taken by under 10 per cent of 16–18-year-olds (IOD 2007). By 2005, however, A Level participation had grown to over 40 per cent of the cohort (DfES 2007a). Moreover, more young people are now passing A Levels – 96.9 per cent in 2007 – and more are attaining the highest grade – 25.3 per cent (JCQ 2007d). The combined effects of an expanding general education route and its continuing use for selection help to explain the very English annual debate about 'standards'. This debate has existed in one form or another since the late 1980s and the factors behind it can be illuminated by a brief periodization of GCSE and A Level developments (see Table 3.1).

What this periodization illustrates is what Lumby and Foskett (2005) refer to as 'turbulence without change', giving rise to a constant and circular debate about standards and the need for reform, resulting in waves of innovation followed by retrenchment. In terms of A Levels, this process is reflected in the fact that individual A Level qualifications have been adapted over the years, but that the basic general education programme of study for 16–19-year-olds – three A Levels – remains relatively unchanged.

Late 1980s – the quiet revolution

The process of A Level modernization began in earnest in the mid-1980s with the introduction of new subjects such as photography and psychology. This was swiftly followed by the appearance of modular syllabuses and

Table 3.1 *GCSEs and A Levels – phases of development and debate*

Period	GCSE development	A Level development	Debates/issues
Late 1980s – the quiet revolution	Introduced in 1986 to replace O Levels and CSEs, leading to rapid rises in attainment rates at 16 and rising participation rates in post-compulsory education.	A Levels are 'modernized', i.e. new subjects, modularization and criterion referenced assessment, but Supplementary AS fails to take off. Experiments with models to combine general and vocational learning.	Relationship between curriculum and qualifications. Proposed solutions to the academic/vocational divide – a more unified or divided system?
Early 1990s – panic and retrenchment	Conservative reaction to the success of GCSE. Retrenchment – introduction of A* grade, reinforcement of A*–C benchmark through tiered papers and performance tables, reduction in course-work.	Development of formal triple-track qualifications system – 'tougher' A Levels, new GNVQs and NVQs for those 'unable' to take A Levels.	GCSE and A Level standards. Critiques of retrench-ment but much more attention paid to the new GNVQs.
Mid 1990s to 2002 – review, reform and crisis	Little focus in this area – gradual introduction of GNVQ Part 1 as an alternatives to GCSE. Increasing use of 5 GCSEs at A*–C grades as a key accountability target for schools.	Focus on A Levels – Dearing Review of 16–19 Qualifications followed by New Labour's *Curriculum 2000* proposals and their implementation. Hargreaves and Tomlinson Reviews of 14–19 education and training (with a focus on A Level standards and manageability).	Part reform of A Levels or whole-system reform? Standards in A Levels. Manageability of *Curriculum 2000* reforms. 'Academic drift' (i.e. vocational qualifications taking on the characteristics of general qualifications to seek 'parity of esteem'.
2002 to date – retrenchment with a 14–19 focus	Relaxation of National Curriculum and more vocational provision 14–16, including GCSEs in vocational subjects and the Increased Flexibility Programme. Proposals for 14–19 Diplomas to replace vocational provision at KS4, reduction of GCSE course-work and focus on 'functional skills' of maths, English and IT.	Proposals to reduce A Level units from 6 to 4, to introduce A* grade and more stretching questions, less coursework and an elective extended project.	Standards in A Levels and GCSEs. Continued calls for the unified Diploma system proposed in the Tomlinson Final Report, despite Government rejection. The implications of a 14–19 phase of education. Major critique of new 14–19 Diplomas – less focus on general education reforms.

examination by course-work (Young and Leney 1997). The changing face of A Levels was not the direct result of government policy but resulted from wider factors. These included the need for A Levels to respond to the increased attainment rates in GCSE and the numbers of learners wanting to participate in post-16 study (Gray et al. 1993) and qualifications developments initiated by the examination boards, supported by wider professional groups (Richardson et al. 1993). While the then Prime Minister, Margaret Thatcher, was prepared to oversee the introduction of GCSEs, she refused to countenance the broadening of A Level programmes and rejected the recommendations of the Higginson Report which proposed that advanced level learners should take five leaner A Levels (DES 1988). Instead, the Government introduced a 'Supplementary A Level' (AS) qualification, to take alongside a two or three A Level programme, but this made little impact.

Early 1990s – panic and retrenchment

By the early 1990s, the Conservative Government felt that the reform of GCSEs and the internal reform of A Levels had gone far enough and inaugurated an era of retrenchment (Spours 1993). The main developments in this period sought to make GCSEs look more like the O Levels they had replaced (that is less assessed course-work, introduction of an A* grade, tiered papers and reinforcement of the A*-C/D-G grade divide). In A Levels, modular experimentation was halted, course-work was reduced and syllabuses were standardized. In addition, under the education and training White Paper (DFE/ED/WO 1991), the Government established a 'triple-track qualifications system' comprising GCSEs and A Levels; the new General National Vocational Qualifications (GNVQs) for full-time learners in schools and colleges; and National Vocational Qualifications (NVQs) for young people and adults in the work-based route (Hodgson and Spours 1997b). As GCSEs and A Levels were being made more distinctive or even 'difficult', the new GNVQ was introduced for those deemed unsuitable for the more 'rigorous' academic track.

Mid-1990s to 2002 – review, reform and crisis

This period of retrenchment soon gave way, due to problems of performance in all three routes in the new triple-track system (see Hodgson and Spours 1997b and 2003 for more detail). Thus a period of review and reform opened in 1995–96 with the government-sponsored but independent Dearing *Review of Qualifications for 16–19 Year Olds* (Dearing 1996) and lasted until the implementation of the *Curriculum 2000* reforms in 2000–2002. The main remit for the Review was to:

- boost post-16 participation and attainment rates;
- improve levels of basic skills;
- to strengthen vocational education;
- make the three qualification tracks more distinctive;
- broaden advanced level study; and
- rationalize the number of qualifications in the National Qualifications Framework.

Despite the fact that Lord Dearing's Review had been set up under a Conservative Government, it was nevertheless influential in New Labour's policy on 16–19 education and training, following their victory in the General Election of 1997. The Report's recommendations for a subsidiary AS, as the first part of A Level study, were incorporated into New Labour's *Curriculum 2000* reforms and influenced the design of the new two-stage AS/A2 A Level qualifications that were introduced in September 2000. The AVCE, which also formed part of the *Curriculum 2000* reforms and was designed to be closely aligned with A Levels to promote mixing of general and vocational study, similarly took ideas from the Dearing Report and from the earlier Review of GNVQs (Capey 1995). The third part of the reform package, and close to Lord Dearing's heart, was the introduction of a new AS qualification in Key Skills that was intended to be taken alongside A Levels and vocational qualifications to broaden advanced level study and to improve skills levels amongst young people. New Labour's adaptation of Lord Dearing's review followed to the letter its 1997 Manifesto commitment to 'support broader A Levels, up-grade vocational qualifications underpinned by rigorous standards and key skills' (Labour Party 1997).

The period of A Level reform continued from September 2000 and came to a close with the Tomlinson Review of A Levels in 2002 (Tomlinson 2002a and 2002b). On the way there were two 'crises' (see Richardson 2007). The first came in 2001 at the end of the first year of implementing the reforms, when there were significant problems over teachers completing the new AS specification, over learner fatigue at the amount of work required under *Curriculum 2000*, over the Key Skills Qualification and over timetabling of the new modular AS examinations. The second much more serious crisis, which was the subject of a torrent of press reporting about 'grade manipulation' in A Levels, took place during the marking of the new qualifications in the summer of 2002. The Government response was to set up a *Curriculum 2000* review process, initially led by David Hargreaves, at the time Chief Executive at QCA, and then by Mike Tomlinson, former Chief Inspector of Her Majesty's Inspectorate. Four detailed reports were produced (Hargreaves 2001a and 2001b; Tomlinson 2002a and 2002b). However, these moves could not save the Minister responsible and Estelle Morris, Secretary of State for Education and Skills, who had become associated with the troubled *Curriculum 2000* reforms, tendered her resignation in October 2002 (see Hodgson and Spours 2003 for more detail).

2002 to date – retrenchment within a 14–19 focus

While the *Curriculum 2000* reforms slowly bedded down over their first two years of implementation and teachers gradually got used to the new processes of teaching and assessment they demanded, the overall perception was that they had not worked well (Ofsted 2003a). Following the second *Curriculum 2000* crisis over grade manipulation, more radical sections of the Labour Government – notably David Miliband who took up a Ministerial portfolio in education in 2002 – seized the initiative to examine a longer-term vision for 14–19 education. This was marked by the proposal in *14–19: Excellence and Opportunity* (DfES 2003) for the establishment of a Working Group on 14–19 Reform chaired by Mike Tomlinson.

As we have seen in Chapter 2, despite Mike Tomlinson's call for a more unified approach to curriculum and qualifications, a new period of retrenchment has, in fact, been taking shape from 2002. This came in the guise of a government-sponsored 14–19 strategy, which started by opening up new opportunities for applied and vocational study for 14–16-year-olds. The full nature of New Labour's retrenchment only became visible following the Government's 14–19 White Paper (DfES 2005a), which rejected Tomlinson's central proposal for a unified diploma system for all 14–19 year olds that would gradually subsume GCSEs and A Levels. Instead, the Government decided to focus on the development of the new vocational 14–19 Diplomas in order to preserve the separate GCSE/A Level route.

What this history suggests is that the process of modernization of GCSEs and A Levels has not been linear. Each wave of reform has been accompanied by a period of retrenchment as a result of pressure from 'traditionalist' forces to retain a separate and selective academic track, while using vocational qualifications to increase participation. After all of the reforms of the last 20 years, the system is larger but its qualifications structure remains relatively unchanged. Each of the qualifications is different to a degree and new ones have been and are being introduced. These 'internal' changes to general education continue apace, but the majority of learner programmes in 2007 look very similar to those of 20 years ago.

PLANNED REFORMS 2005–2013

As we have seen in Chapter 2, there are a number of key messages running through the Government's White Paper *14–19 Education and Skills*, the document that announced the Government's strategy for this phase. The overarching aim is to raise levels of participation and achievement because of concerns about being 'close to the bottom of the OECD league table for participation among 17 year-olds' (DfES 2005a: 10). In the area of general education, the Government was adamant to retain existing academic qualifications 'because GCSEs and A levels are well understood' (DfES 2005a: 12), while 'continuing to transform standards in the basics' (DCSF 2007b) and to strengthen GCSEs and A Levels 'to stretch the most able' (DfES 2005a: 12). In the case of A Levels, there was also a desire to 'help universities to differentiate between candidates' (DfES 2005a: 61). These reforms were to take effect from September 2008.

A Levels

The main aims of the A Level changes are to correct what the Government saw as dysfunctional features of their *Curriculum 2000* reforms. They were concerned to reduce the negative impact of modular testing on the experience of A Level learning and to provide 'stretch and challenge for our brightest students' (DfES 2005a: 59).

The *Curriculum 2000* reforms had led to a marked increase in the numbers achieving an A grade at A Level, with the complaint from some universities that selection was proving more difficult. DfES statistics showed that there was a rising trend in examination attainment in the highest grades. In 1995–6, 6.1 per cent of A Level candidates attained three A Levels at grade A, and this rose slightly to 7.4 per cent over the five years prior to the *Curriculum 2000* reforms. Since 2001–2, following the introduction of the new AS/A2 qualifications, achievement of three A grades rose more rapidly from 7.4 to 10.7 per cent of A Level candidates in 2005–6. How far this constitutes a serious problem is open to debate. The difficulty of differentiation between A Level candidates affects very few 'selector' universities and departments, but these are the ones with a great deal of cultural leverage, hence they have a strong voice in the policy process.

To address the problems associated with *Curriculum 2000*, the Government proposed to reduce the number of units within A Level specifications from six to four, to limit the amount of assessment in these qualifications and to offer more space to study a subject in greater depth. University admissions tutors had voiced concerns that *Curriculum 2000* was not adequately preparing young people for higher education study (Wilde and Wright 2007). Moreover, learners and teachers had complained about the quality of teaching and learning (Fisher 2007), the number of examinations resulting from a six-module award and the difficulty of completing the course at AS Level prior to the summer examination period (Hodgson and Spours 2003). A related change is the introduction into the A2 of more 'stretching questions' (DCSF 2007c), which means fewer short answer questions, more extended writing and more synoptic questions, as well as an A* grade. This latter grade has been designed to be awarded only to that small proportion of young people able to attain an overall A grade at A Level with very high achievement in the A2 units: AS results will not contribute to the A* grade. In addition, course-work is only allowable in a minority of subjects (for example art and design and PE) and all candidates will have to demonstrate a high quality of written communication.

GCSEs

The Government's 2002 Green Paper talked of GCSEs moving from a school-leaving examination to a 'progress check'. This suggested a declining role for a 16+ examination at a time when more young people were staying on in education and training. Associated with this was the idea of 'acceleration', with students taking qualifications early, represented in the slogan 'stage not age'. However, the 2005 14–19 White Paper emphasized the continued role of GCSE as a 16+ threshold by asserting that it was widely recognized by parents and respected internationally and should, therefore, remain. The role of GCSE as an important educational milestone was further strengthened by changes to performance tables to include a higher threshold for the 5A*–C benchmark by including maths and English GCSE. This focus on improving basic skills can also be seen in the proposals to incorporate the functional skills of English, mathematics and ICT into the revised GCSEs in these areas. Another important change to these qualifications, referred to as 'toughening GCSEs' (DCFS 2007d), is the replacement of course-work by 'controlled assessments'.[7]

The growing rigour of GCSEs will be offset by expanding the range of GCSEs in vocational subjects and by the possibility of developing more unitized specifications so that learners can re-sit parts of the new, more externally assessed qualification. The majority of the revised GCSE specifications will be available from September 2008 for first teaching in 2009.

The 14–19 reforms in relation to GCSEs could lead to four inter-related effects. First, they reinforce a 16+ divide and call into question a coherent 14–19 phase. Second, they can be seen as part of the move to make the general route more selective and are likely to lead to a reduction in a proportion of young people gaining the new threshold of 5*A–C at 16. Third, they constitute part of the Government's 'choice agenda', in which a more diverse range of qualifications is available for 14–16-year-olds. Finally, they are likely to make a difference to pedagogy with more focus than ever on learning for examinations.

Functional skills

Functional skills are the latest in a long line of qualifications designed to improve young people's basic skills in English, mathematics and ICT because of constant complaints from employers – British Chamber of Commerce (Frost 2007), Federation of Small Businesses (Undy 2007) and the Institute of Directors (IOD 2007). Over the last 20 years, there have been repeated initiatives in this area under different banners – core skills, key skills, basic skills, essential skills and now, finally, functional skills, all of which either never saw the light of day or proved highly problematic (see Hodgson and Spours 2002). The DCSF describes functional skills as 'those core elements of English, maths and ICT that provide an individual with the essential knowledge, skills and understanding that will enable them to operate confidently, effectively and independently at life and at work' (DCSF 2007d).

As we have discussed earlier, all young people taking GCSE English, mathematics and ICT will have to study the functional skills as part of their course. Functional skills also constitute a compulsory component of all the new Diploma qualifications (see Chapter 4) and are part of the national 14–19 Entitlement. They are being developed at three levels and will bring both key skills and the adult literacy and numeracy skills into one set of standards. The new qualifications are currently being piloted with the aim to have them universally ready for delivery in 2010.

Two recent evaluation reports (CLL 2007; Greenwood et al. 2007) provide useful insights into these qualifications. The former, having evaluated pilots, concluded that while the design of the new qualifications appeared to be broadly workable, there was very low awareness amongst teachers and lecturers about the new initiative. The latter report, whose major remit was to evaluate the predecessors of functional skills in order to inform the development and implementation of the new qualifications, was much more critical. It concluded that functional skills were not seen as a high priority within the 14–19 reforms, that schools were less experienced and engaged than colleges and that there would need to be a long-term strategic commitment from the Government in order to make the new reforms work. Finally, the researchers raised a concern about the effects of the functional skills on achievement rates in GCSE English and mathematics and highlighted, yet again, the issue of whether young people would be able to transfer these skills effectively to the workplace.

The Extended Project

The Tomlinson Final Report envisaged all 14–19-year-olds being required to undertake a major piece of work related to their study programme in order to develop their learning skills and to motivate them to pursue a topic of their choice in depth (Working Group for 14–19 Reform 2004a). The Government borrowed this idea for the Extended Project, with the aim of offering opportunities for candidates 'to take responsibility either for an individual task or a defined task within a group project' and 'to develop and improve their own learning and performance as critical, reflective and independent learners' (QCA, WAG and CEA 2006: 3). This award, which can take different forms, ranging from an extended essay to a performance, will be internally graded A*–E and subject to external moderation. Candidates will need to present their work.

Colleges of the University of Cambridge, responding to a UCAS/DfES Curriculum Development Group exercise in 2005, broadly supported the Extended Project because of the skills that it would foster in university applicants. However, they raised concerns about whether it could be proved to be the candidate's own work and suggested that it would only be used as part of an interview process.

The Extended Project currently has limited scope within general education, being confined to use within the Diplomas and, on an elective basis, for students undertaking A Levels. It is not available for learners in general education below Level 3, nor is it on offer to learners on vocational programmes other than the Diplomas, although there are some pilots taking place in this area. It appears, therefore, that relatively few learners will experience the Extended Project in its current form.

International Baccalaureate, Pre-U and International GCSE

In December 2006, the DfES wrote to all local authorities in England asking them to nominate one suitable institution in their area to deliver the International Baccalaureate (IB) in either 2009 or 2010 to ensure 'that it is available in a maintained school or college in every area of the country' (Coles 2006). The IB Diploma Programme for students aged 16–19 is offered in 1,597 schools and colleges worldwide, 101 of which are in the UK.[8] It is described by the International Baccalaureate Organisation (IBO) as a 'challenging two-year programme of international education', which contains a common core and six subject groups. The compulsory core comprises an extended essay, theory of knowledge and community action service and is seen as 'central to the philosophy of the Diploma Programme'. The six subjects, three of which are normally studied at 'higher level', with the other three at 'standard level', are chosen from six broad groupings: for example Group 3 Individuals and societies, Group 5 Mathematics and computer science.[9] In comparison with a standard A Level programme, therefore, the IB is considerably broader, more holistic in curriculum terms and more structured. It is highly regarded but is considered to be a tough option because of its demands in terms of breadth (Kearns 2004), particularly the requirement of two modern foreign languages (Hill 2003). It is also costly to deliver and is currently offered in about a quarter of local authorities in England.

It is significant that it was the then Prime Minister, Tony Blair, who announced the Government's intention to extend access to the IB to all areas of England, promising £2.5m funding to make this possible (BBC 2006). The issue for local authorities, who have been charged with making this development happen, is both finding schools or colleges willing to make the investment required to offer the IB and ensuring that it has the staff qualified to teach the award. There is also a question about whether 16–19-year-olds, who have traditionally seen post-16 study as a time to specialize and to drop 'difficult' subjects, such as mathematics and modern foreign languages, will be as eager to opt into an IB programme as their parents or politicians might want them to be. Moreover, as Chapter 6 points out, providing additional funding for one institution in a local authority area – particularly money which might be spent elsewhere – causes considerable resentment and is not helpful when local authorities are trying to promote institutional collaboration rather than stoking the fires of competition.

So why has the Government been so keen to introduce the IB? First, it is about political expediency. The IB is one answer to the small number of politically influential higher education institutions, which claim that the current A Level system does not allow them to distinguish between the brightest candidates. Second, it can be seen as a response to those in the education profession and beyond who argue that A Level programmes are still too narrow and that the Government should have adopted the Tomlinson Diploma system to provide more breadth at advanced level. Third, it might be seen as part of an inclusion agenda – the state school system should be offering the same kind of opportunities to its learners as the independent sector. For all these reasons, the former Prime Minister's announcement on the IB might be considered as a politically astute move and further evidence of the pursuit of a 'choice' and individual entitlement agenda to head off criticisms which might force the Government to think more radically about whole-system reform.

There are two other qualifications in the general education track that are not endorsed by government and might be seen as alternatives or even competitors to GCSEs and A Levels: the International GCSE (iGCSE) and the Pre-U qualification, both of which are being actively supported by the independent school sector. The former, developed in 1988 by the University of Cambridge International Examination (CIE) Board, acts as an alternative to GCSE for 14–16-year-olds. The qualification is now offered by two awarding bodies and is proving popular with independent schools, particularly in mathematics (Lucas 2008). State schools are not currently funded to offer iGCSEs, but some would like the opportunity to.[10] The Pre-U is a newer qualification, designed by CIE, as an alternative to A levels for 16–19-year-olds. The programme, comprising three full linear A Levels, an independent research report and a course in global perspectives, was available for teaching in September 2008.

What the interest in these endorsed and unendorsed alternatives to GCSEs and A Levels demonstrates is an increasing dissatisfaction in both the independent school sector and, to a lesser degree, in state schools and colleges, with the traditional qualifications on offer in the general education track in England. Whether the proposed 14–19 reforms will stem the flight to these alternative qualifications and silence the growing criticism of A Levels and GCSEs remains to be seen.

Foundation Learning Tier

Right at the other end of the spectrum, in terms of political interest, lies the Foundation Learning Tier (FLT). It was developed in relative obscurity as a response to the Government's focus on Level 2 attainment and its failure to implement the more inclusive aspects of the Tomlinson Report's recommendations – that is a unified diploma system from Entry Level upwards. The FLT is being designed to 'establish an inclusive curriculum offer at Entry Level and Level 1 for learners from age 14 upwards' (QCA/LSC 2005: 1). From the publicly available documentation on government agency websites and policy documents, it is difficult to establish exactly what the FLT is and how it articulates with the rest of the 14–19 reforms, despite the fact that a 'phased rollout' commenced in September 2007 (DCSF 2007e). What is clear is that the FLT will be programmatic and includes skills for life and work, vocational subject-based learning and personal and social development. In an issue of OCR *Diploma Watch*, the FLT appeared to be more clearly defined by what it was not than by what it was:

> *Subject-based qualifications at Level 1 will not be included ... Not all ICT and languages qualifications will be included ... Nor is it likely that largely job-specific qualifications will be included ... (OCR 2006: 1).*

What this suggests is that it is quite discrete from other areas of learning and, if anything, should be considered as part of vocational or pre-vocational education rather than general education. Does this mean that learners below a certain level will not be considered eligible to take general education programmes from 14+?

There will undoubtedly be practitioner support for the FLT because, as a QCA leaflet states, it will serve the needs of '14–19-year-olds for whom GCSEs are not appropriate, adults with skills gaps and adults or young people with learning difficulties and/or disabilities' (QCA/LSC 2007). However, its association with this client group, its focus on remedying deficits and its 'afterthought' feel are not likely to make the FLT an attractive option to learners, parents or employers.

Three new Diplomas

Finally, we cannot complete a description of planned reforms to 14–19 general education in England without mentioning the three additional 14–19 Diploma lines in science, languages and the humanities which were unexpectedly announced in October 2007 by the new ministerial team at the DCSF, led by the Secretary of State Ed Balls. Originally confined to 14 vocational sectors, the introduction of the three new lines now brings general education subjects into the Diploma suite, albeit at a later stage than their vocational counterparts. In Chapters 4 and 6 we discuss the practical and political implications of this move. We also ask whether this announcement signals a significant step towards the development of the unified diploma framework recommended by the Tomlinson Final Report, or whether it is simply a desire to shore-up the current 14 Diploma lines which have had a chequered start in life. What was abundantly clear from Ed Balls' speech in October 2007, however, was that the introduction of Diplomas into general education does not mean the imminent demise of GCSEs and A levels (DCSF 2007f).

CONCLUSION – FOUR PERSPECTIVES ON THE REFORM OF GENERAL EDUCATION

Viewed from a distance, the Government's latest reforms to the general education track do not appear to substantially alter either the shape or function of this part of the 14–19 system. It remains dominated by A Levels and GCSE subjects; its selection function continues; there is a strong divide at the age of 16 marked by high stakes national examinations; and post-16 it remains elective and narrow in curricular terms. In fact, seasoned observers of the English system will note that, despite the deliberations about broader programmes of study that took place as part of the Tomlinson Review, the Government decided not to go down the baccalaureate road.

At the national level, this latest set of reforms to general education might be seen as part of an historical pattern of the opening up of participation, followed by a period of retrenchment. As in 1992, the Government used changes to assessment to restore confidence in the selective ability of GCSEs and A Levels. In 2007, this move was an admission that the partial reform of advanced level study through the *Curriculum 2000* reforms had, in fact, failed to produce breadth or confidence in standards. Moreover, the Government succumbed to pressure from employers and higher education tutors to stem the increasing levels of attainment associated with the modular AS/A2 qualifications. A vital part of this 'retrenchment' process in general education is to put in place alternative vocational/applied qualifications. What lies behind these changes are political rather than educational motives, although educational arguments will be deployed. For example, the QCA states that less modular assessment and course-work will provide more space for the type of in-depth study required by universities (QCA 2007b).

From a practitioner perspective, on the other hand, the reforms being introduced in September 2008 represent yet another major upheaval. Most practitioners have little idea of the proposed changes in GCSEs and A Levels because attention is currently focused on delivery of the new 14–19 Diplomas. While some of the reforms – for example, the reduction in course-work requirements and the number of modular examinations – are likely to be mildly welcomed by some subject teachers, others may regret feeling pressurized to teach to the test. The FLT is such an unknown quantity at the moment that it is difficult to gauge how it will be viewed by practitioners. They are likely to welcome courses which motivate learners excluded from the mainstream curriculum, but will be concerned about its credibility and progression opportunities – anxieties that have surfaced time and again since the experiments with CPVE in the mid-1980s. Within the disparate general education reform package some areas are likely to prove more problematic than others. A leading candidate is the functional skills because of the chequered history of earlier qualifications of this type, such as key skills (see Hodgson and Spours 2002). Another is the new 5A*–C GCSE benchmark, including English and mathematics, which will reduce the proportion of young people 'passing' their GCSEs and increase the numbers who consider themselves a failure at 16+. For school and college curriculum managers, September 2008 looks like being a bit of a nightmare with so many changes taking place at the same time, a point made forcibly by teacher unions and professional associations (for example NUT 2007).

Finally, it is interesting to speculate how changes to general education will affect learners. Here we suggest at least two different outcomes. The reforms were designed principally with high attainers in mind and these young people are likely to welcome more space for learning in Year 12, an opportunity to specialize in an area of interest through the Extended Project and even the possibility of taking the IB. The greatest beneficiaries will be those able to attain the new A* grade at A Level and to move to the front of the queue for entry to highly selective university courses. These learners will be largely from the independent school sector. On the other hand, those at the other end of the spectrum – low achievers, the disaffected and those with special needs – will find themselves increasingly detached from mainstream general education, either channelled into the FLT or programmes such as Entry to Employment. Many of those in between will either see little difference or may find themselves struggling with the revised GCSEs and A Levels and tempted to take the new but untried 14–19 Diplomas. While the A Level regime is undoubtedly going to be more difficult, the jury is still out on GCSE and Key Stage 4. Creating a more accessible and motivating general education for 14–16-year-olds will depend on the extent to which learners opt for mixed programmes of study combining general and applied learning and whether this involves the majority of students. If the take-up of applied and vocational options remains the preserve of lower achievers, as has been the case in the past, then the reforms will have taken selection, which is powerful at 16, down to the age of 14.

The overall effect of the Government's approach to the general track in 14–19 education in England is to place more pressure on the broad vocational and work-based routes as they are expected to absorb 'refugees' from 'tougher' GCSEs and 'strengthened' A Levels. As we will see in the following chapters, it is academic qualifications which continue to shape not only vocational education but also the 14–19 system as a whole.

NOTES

[1] When the National Curriculum was first introduced in 1988 there was a greater degree of compulsion, including the requirement to study a modern foreign language, art, design and technology, history and geography.

[2] In Scotland, the examination system is somewhat different, with young people at this age taking Standard Grade qualifications in a number of subjects. In this chapter we focus primarily on the English qualifications system because it dominates the UK field in terms of numbers of young people and still has a strong determining influence on Wales and Northern Ireland.

[3] This figure varies across different parts of England, with local authorities in the North having lower full-time participation rates than those in the South (DfES 2007a).

[4] This figure includes both traditional AS/A2 A Level qualifications and applied A Levels, which used to be called Advanced Vocational Certificates of Education (AVCE).

[5] Under this reform, which began in September 2000, all A Levels were split into two three-unit blocks – Advanced Subsidiary (AS) and A2 – with the first part normally taken in the first year of study and the second, dependent part in the second year. The AS is set at a lower level than the A2 but has the same number of grade points attached to it – both scores are aggregated to achieve the final A Level grade.

[6] A DCSF (2007b) consultation document published in December 2007 proposes the division of the QCA into two separate organizations: the Office of Qualifications and Examinations Regulation, which report directly to Parliament, and a development agency for curriculum,

assessment and qualifications.

[7] From 2009, all attainments in GCSEs will be measured through controlled assessment in which there will be varying degrees of external control over task setting, task taking and task marking (QCA 2007a).

[8] www.ibo.org/country/GB/

[9] www.ibo.org/diploma

[10] http://news.bbc.co.uk/2/hi/uk_news/education/4263600.stm

chapter 4

THE 14-19 DIPLOMAS

DIPLOMAS – A HIGH PROFILE AND RISKY VENTURE

In November 2006, Alan Johnson, then Secretary of State for Education and Skills, described 14-19 Diplomas as representing 'the most radical educational development taking place probably anywhere in the world' and a 'thrilling development' (Johnson 2006). By March 2007, however, he was on record as confessing 'Things could go horribly wrong, particularly as we are keeping A Levels and GCSEs' (BBC 2007a). These two seemingly contradictory statements reflect the paradox of the Diplomas. The Government has invested virtually everything in the power of these qualifications to transform 14-19 education and training and they constituted its main response to the Tomlinson Report (Working Group on 14-19 Reform 2004a).

As we have explained in the previous chapter, the Government was not prepared to bring GCSEs and A Levels into a single framework, choosing instead to focus on the reform of broad vocational qualifications as the main means of engaging learners in the 14-16 curriculum and raising levels of post-16 participation. Thus we see politicians and policy-makers hyping-up a reform in order to demonstrate their radical credentials, only to realize that they could have made a terrible mistake. In his first statement, the then Secretary of State could be seen as a typical politician, well on-message. In his second comment, he was reflecting not only his own private thoughts, but also those of many, if not most, policy-makers and practitioners. The public concerns about the Diplomas prompted an enquiry by the House of Commons Education and Skills Committee, which reported in May 2007, even before the Diploma specifications had been published (HoC 2007). The Committee highlighted concerns that the long-term role of the Diplomas could be jeopardized unless these awards were reviewed alongside A Levels in 2008/9. The Tomlinson argument for the simultaneous reform of general and vocational education had come back to haunt the Government.

The October 2007 decision by Ed Balls, the then Secretary of State at the new Department of Schools, Children and Families (DSCF), to introduce three new lines of Diplomas in science, humanities and languages changed the picture somewhat because the Diplomas could be seen to be shifting closer to the Tomlinson proposals for a unified Diploma system. However, as long as A Levels remain as discrete qualifications, it is difficult to see Diplomas becoming what the Secretary of State for DCSF described as the 'qualification of choice' for young people (DCSF 2007a).

In this chapter, we locate the development of the Diplomas as the latest in a long line of 'middle-track' qualifications. The first 14 lines were originally termed 'Specialized Diplomas', a name which, in our view, more accurately denoted their underlying vocational conception and function. In outlining this history, we reflect on the difficulties that vocational middle-track qualifications have faced, wedged between a large and culturally dominant academic track and a small but attractive apprenticeship route. Our main argument is that the future of the Diplomas, as broad vocational or even more applied qualifications, will be affected not only by their design, structure, content and assessment, important though these are, but by issues of learner and end-user demand. As such, we do not see the Diplomas making a great impact on 14–19 education and certainly not on the scale claimed by government. In addition, we discuss some of the implementation issues that emerged as a result of politically determined timescales for the introduction of the new qualifications. We single out for comment the decision to introduce an entirely new award with an employer-led design process, rather than gradually building on existing qualifications in a more inclusive way. We conclude the chapter by suggesting that there are three ways of viewing the Diplomas at this point and identify strategies that might be employed to ensure that the new awards play a positive role in the short-term and can, in the long-term, become part of a more holistic approach to reforming 14–19 education as a whole.

BROAD VOCATIONAL QUALIFICATIONS – LESSONS FROM HISTORY

We have argued in Chapter 2 that ministers tend not to consider reform within its broader historical context because they want to be associated with bold new ideas, delivering new initiatives and capturing images of the future. They tend to neglect the past, unwilling to learn lessons from previous policy-making (Raffe and Spours 2007). We consider it important, therefore, not to do the same and to examine the genesis of the Diplomas within their wider historical and policy context. This is particularly important with these awards because the Government has deliberately stressed their new and different nature.

The history of broad vocational qualifications in England spans more than two decades with three major awards that stand out: General National Vocational Qualifications (GNVQs), Advanced Vocational Certificates of Education (AVCEs) and Business and Technology Educational Council (BTEC) National Diplomas. What all of these broad vocational qualifications had in common was that they were introduced to respond to rising levels of full-time post-16 participation in a divided qualifications system (Hodgson and Spours 1997a). Of these, BTEC National Diplomas demand attention because of the way they gradually became accepted by employers and even higher education throughout the late 1980s and early 1990s and have become a durable part of the vocational qualifications landscape, despite the indifference or even hostility of successive governments (Williams 1999).

Broad vocational qualifications have occupied what might be termed the 'middle track'. In this location, they have experienced a mixture of success and failure. Their successes include being regarded as 'motivational' qualifications for the disengaged (Williams 1999; Bathmaker 2001), contributing to full-time 16–19 participation rates and providing a relatively small but significant alternative route into certain parts of higher education. Their weaknesses, however, outweighed their strengths.

First, they were never able to escape the shadow of A Levels. The most capable learners continued to take these awards and the very success of broad vocational qualifications in their 'motivational' role meant that they were seen as an 'alternative' curriculum (Spours 1997; Williams 1999). Second, GNVQs and AVCEs were designed for post-16 programmes in schools and colleges and they have singularly failed to articulate with apprenticeships and work-based learning, another potential source of prestige (FEDA/IOE/Nuffield 1997). The third weakness concerned assessment. Both GNVQs and AVCEs became weighed down by NVQ competence-derived assessment methodology, contributing to mediocre attainment and learner instrumentalism (Bates 1997; Torrance 2006; Ecclestone 2006). For AVCEs, the assessment issue became even more acute because, despite their lower status, it was more difficult to achieve high grades in them than in A Levels (Savory et al. 2003). A related issue for both qualifications, although more prevalent with GNVQ, was constant government interference both with their labelling and with their design, processes which compounded the problem of their low visibility and take-up by learners. Hence their fifth weakness, particularly in the case of AVCE, was their relative lack of recognition by either higher education (Hodgson et al. 2005a) or employers.

This balance of strengths and weaknesses arising from historical analysis points to significant challenges facing the Diplomas. History teaches us that politically and ideologically inspired qualifications reform which deliberately seeks to provide a full-time alternative to A Levels does not work. Of the broad vocational qualifications developed over the last two decades, only BTEC National Diplomas, which were not designed by government, were established more slowly with wide support from employers, practitioners and later from higher education providers, proved to be enduring and relatively successful.

In the subsequent discussion, we explore the extent to which the Diplomas are subject to the same forces and are likely to follow the same trajectory as their troubled predecessors. To do this we first describe the Diplomas and then examine their position within the national qualifications system.

WHAT ARE THE DIPLOMAS?

As we saw in Chapter 1, at the heart of the national 14–19 Entitlement lie the new 'employer-designed' Diplomas of which there will now be 17 lines offered at Levels 1 to 3 of the National Qualifications Framework. The first five lines – IT; society, health and development; construction and the built environment; engineering; creative and media – will be available from September 2008. A further five – land-based and environmental; manufacturing; hair and beauty studies; business administration and finance; and hospitality – will be offered from September 2009. These will be joined by four further lines – public services; sport and leisure; retail; and travel and tourism – in September 2010. The three additional Diploma lines in science, languages and humanities will be introduced by 2011.

Ministers intend that the Diplomas should provide 'an exciting, stretching and relevant programme of learning for young people of all backgrounds and abilities' (DfES 2006c: 3) and should prepare them for life and work. It is claimed that the Diplomas will achieve this by their blend of general and applied learning in 'real world environments' (each Diploma has to include at least 10 days of learning in a work setting) and the fact that they have been designed by both employers and educators.

The Diploma qualification

The 14 original Diplomas[1] were described as 'composite awards' with a common basic design comprising three 'components' (DfES 2006d: 10):

- *Principal Learning*, which is sector related and mandatory, is intended to 'develop knowledge, understanding and skills relevant to a broad economic sector, using realistic contexts and leading edge sector relevant materials';
- *Generic Learning*, which is again mandatory, 'will ensure that all Diploma students cover common skills essential to successful learning and future employment'. It includes personal learning and thinking skills (PLTS), a project, work experience and the functional skills of English, mathematics and ICT.
- *Additional/Specialist Learning*, which will vary from Diploma line to Diploma line, consists of units and qualifications from the NQF, which 'will allow learners to tailor their programme according to their interests and aspirations and may include further specialisation, or complementary studies'.

The size of the Diploma varies at the different levels and is measured in what are called 'guided learning hours' (GLH). At Level 1, the 'Foundation' Diploma requires 600 GLH, which is broadly comparable to the amount of study needed for four to five GCSEs. The Level 2 'Higher' Diploma asks for 800 GLH (comparable to seven GCSEs), while the Level 3 'Advanced' Diploma is the largest of all at 1,080 GLH, which is deemed comparable to a three and a half GCE A Level programme (Lipsett 2007). At Level 3, a smaller 'Progression Award' will be available with a volume of 720 GLH, equivalent to a two A Level programme.[2]

Just as the volume of the Diploma differs at the three levels, so too do the proportions of the three components within the award. Generic Learning takes up a larger part of the programme at Level 1 compared with the other two levels because of the need to offer more skill-based learning to aid progression. Principal Learning is bigger at Level 3 than the levels below in order to include more sector-related study.

Unlike previous broad vocational qualifications, which had different variants for pre-16 and post-16 learners to recognize their different levels of maturity, the design of the Diplomas is the same whether they are taken by 14–16-year-olds as part of compulsory education, or by 16–19-year-olds in post-compulsory learning. However, the majority of 14–16-year-olds would be expected to be on Level 1 or Level 2 programmes, with those at 16+ mainly taking Level 3 awards. As we will see later, this particular design feature poses a number of challenges.

While adhering to the overall Diploma template described above, each line of Diplomas takes a different approach to content, based on vocational sector requirements as determined by the Diploma Development Partnership (DDP) appointed by the relevant Sector Skills Council (SSC).

All Diplomas contain both external and internal assessment, although the proportions of these will vary according to Diploma line and level. In order to achieve the Diploma, learners need to pass all three components (Principal, Generic and Additional/Specialist Learning). To recognize the importance of the Functional Skills of English, mathematics and IT, passing the Diploma also includes gaining these three qualifications at the same level as the Diploma, except for Level 3 where it is only necessary to gain Functional Skills at Level 2. Not all parts of Generic Learning are separately assessed. PLTS, for example, are integrated into Principal Learning and are recorded on the Diploma Transcript. The Diploma has an overall grade based on Principal Learning and the Extended Project. Elements which make up Specialist/Additional Learning and which are recorded on the Transcript may or may not be graded, depending on whether they are competence-based or not.

So to what extent do Diplomas differ from earlier broad vocational qualifications? The answer is, to a degree. One of the major differences is that they have been designed from the start as 14–19 rather than 16–19 qualifications. The Diplomas are more strongly programmatic, broader and more flexibly tailored to individual need than earlier middle-track awards, in that they potentially include a mix of academic and vocational study as well as a strong element of generic learning. It is possible, for example, to take an A Level as part of Additional/Specialist Learning, although this is not a requirement. Earlier broad vocational awards, such as GNVQ, did include a weak form of generic learning – key skills – but did not require an extended project, nor was it possible to take an academic qualification as part of the award. In addition, it is claimed that Diplomas will be more strongly work-related because of the 10-day work experience requirement in Generic Learning and the fact that a minimum of 50 per cent of Principal

Learning 'must be concerned with the application of knowledge and skills through tasks, problems and situations that are related to work in that sector' (QCA 2007c: 4). Taken together, these three differences could be seen as assets in terms of progression, skill development, learner motivation, pedagogy and the promotion of a broader curriculum and it is undoubtedly these features that excite the policy advocates of the new awards.

However, these features also confirm the Diploma's location as a middle-track qualification, between dominant GCSEs and A Levels on one side and strongly vocational qualifications and apprenticeships on the other. The very breadth and flexibility of the Diplomas have contributed to concerns about their identity and function, begging the question 'What are the Diplomas?'

Aims and purposes

The following quotations, from government documents and official statements, illustrate the multiple purposes the Diplomas are intended to serve:

> They have been created to provide a real alternative to traditional education and qualifications. (DfES 2006d: 1)

> Because of their unique design, Diplomas are equally suitable for the most able pupils preparing for demanding university courses; for young people who find the existing education system doesn't suit them and for those who want to go straight into work after leaving school. (DfES 2006e: 1)

> Diplomas are intended to provide 'something which is broader, which develops people's cognitive skills and which is not just training for a specific occupation. So that is the key purpose [of the Diplomas]'. (Coles, cited in HoC 2007: 15)

The House of Commons Education and Skills Committee, reporting on 14-19 Diplomas, captured the major issue of definition and purpose of the new awards by commenting: 'It has not always been clear to what extent the new programmes are intended to be vocational, or applied, or to serve a more general education purpose'. It went on to state that 'the Government's own standpoint on this issue appears to have changed over time' (HoC 2007: 13). As we have noted earlier, this is reflected in the changing name of the new awards from 'Specialized Diplomas' in February 2005 to 'Diplomas' in March 2007 (DfES 2007d). One of our interviewees suggested the reasoning behind this movement:

What they [the Diplomas] have done, is that they've shifted their ground so that they are now, rather than being aligned quite closely to apprenticeships and industry/occupational needs, they are now very closely aligned to GCSEs and A Levels, in an attempt to, if you like, guarantee the rigour and standard of those qualifications. (PA 14)

Diplomas are thus meant to provide a major part of a reformed 14–19 curriculum that is intended to motivate young people to participate and achieve in education or training up to the age of 19. In this sense, their fundamental purpose is no different from their predecessor broad vocational qualifications. In this role, they operate primarily as full-time programmes of study and as 'alternatives' to academic A Levels and GCSEs. In addition, both the DfES and QCA have attempted to justify the role of the Diplomas for 14–16-year-olds by asserting that presently there are no alternatives to academic GCSEs other than vocational training programmes (QCA submission to HoC 2007). This is inaccurate. Schools up and down the land, as part of increased flexibility encouraged in Key Stage 4, following the 14–19 Green Paper (DfES 2002), have introduced BTEC First Diplomas, ASDAN awards and other forms of certification for 14–16-year-olds.

The Government's approach to the Diplomas was underpinned by two basic assumptions. It was asserted that academic qualifications did not require major reform and that alternatives had to be created for learners who could not succeed in them. It was also claimed that there were serious problems with vocational qualifications provision, suggesting the need for an entirely new suite of awards. This was to lead to what we will argue was an excessive investment in a single initiative. As we have suggested in Chapter 2, the reluctance of the Government to reform the qualifications system as a whole has meant that Diplomas, as the major flagship of the Government's 14–19 reform agenda, have had to play a whole series of roles and to serve a multitude of purposes. The recent history of broad vocational qualifications suggests that it is difficult to design a single set of awards to meet this wide range of needs without compromising one or more of its aims. In the case of both GNVQs (FEDA/IOE 1997) and AVCEs (Savory et al. 2003), this led to qualifications which were neither sufficiently vocational to be highly valued by employers nor sufficiently 'academic' to be fully accepted by universities. The lesson here is that confusions about purpose fundamentally undermine external recognition and value.

PROBLEMS OF MIDDLE-TRACK LOCATION

Diplomas, GCSEs and A Levels

Problems of identity and purpose appear inevitable with middle-track qualifications because they end up being defined by the tracks on either side of them and, in particular by A Levels. This dilemma is perhaps best illustrated through a brief story of how Diplomas have moved from one identity to another over a period of two years.

As we have already shown, in 2005 they were conceived as an alternative to GCSEs and A Levels as part of a reformed 14–19 curriculum, which was intended to give learners more choice of study. At this point, the Government was aware of the need to provide a strongly vocational curriculum designed by employers, which it hoped would prove attractive to both young people and to end-users. To this end, it set up DDPs to design the Principal Learning component of the first five Specialized Diploma lines, as they were then called. The name 'Specialized Diploma' indicated clearly that these were intended to be vocational awards. During the development process, all DDPs were very concerned to ensure that the Diplomas, particularly at Level 3, were viewed as high-quality alternatives to A Levels. In engineering, in particular, it appears that the engineering DDP was aware of the danger of competing with A Levels and designed the content of the Diploma to emphasize parity of esteem in order to attract students away from the academic track. Concerns about parity of esteem spread quickly across all DDPs throughout 2006. By 2007, even the then Secretary of State, Alan Johnson, admitted 'There is a danger of the Diplomas becoming if you like the secondary modern compared to the grammar' (BBC 2007a). By March of that year, it was decided that the term 'specialized' should be dropped and that the new awards should simply be known as Diplomas.

This concern about the identity of the new qualifications has been compounded by universities' initial lukewarm reception of the Diplomas. In a survey commissioned by ACS International Schools, only four in ten universities viewed the Diploma as a good alternative to A Levels, with the majority of respondents commenting they thought the new qualification would result in a 'two-tier system' (BBC 2007b). The co-existence of the new awards alongside existing A Levels and GCSEs has thus already produced two problematical outcomes. It quickly deflected the Diplomas from their original strongly vocational mission into yet another middle-track award and, in this location, the Diplomas are already seen as losers in comparison with the dominant academic qualifications.

Diplomas, vocational qualifications and the work-based route

The vacillations in terms of role and identity have also inevitably affected the relationship of Diplomas with the work-based route and other vocational qualifications. At the time of writing, they are seen as a full-time route to but not the actual qualifications basis of apprenticeship (QCA 2007c).

It is almost certain that Diplomas will replace the more school-based GNVQ, AVCE and GCSEs in vocational subjects. It is not at all certain, however, how they will be able, or even should, supplant the more sharply vocational BTEC and CGLI awards, no matter how much ministers may desire this. These awards straddle college-based and work-based learning programmes and, in some cases, serve as the technical certificate component of apprenticeship frameworks. Their role was mentioned by several interviewees as being different from the Diplomas, with one remarking:

> If you took a long hard-nosed look at the Diplomas and much of BTEC, you'd find it difficult to sweep away a huge amount ... because of the level of occupational specificity ... they'd be additional to and complementary to the Diploma offer. (PA 5)

Precisely because of this, there is considerable resistance in FE colleges to any award that might threaten well-established and highly regarded BTEC provision. Colleges have recent memories of embarking on new middle-track awards, such as AVCEs, only to return to BTEC National Diplomas a few years later. Moreover, awarding bodies, such as Edexcel, OCR and CGLI, are only likely to surrender their tried and tested qualifications if Diplomas are able to subsume some of their specialist vocational functions. It appears that 14–19 Pathfinders may be finding ways of bringing a BTEC approach into certain Level 3 Diplomas (for example creative and media), but this may not be possible across all Diploma lines. At this point, it would be a risky and controversial strategy to privilege Diplomas over existing vocational awards by cutting off state funding for the latter.

In addition, there is no guarantee that employers will recognize the Diplomas to the extent that young people will detect strong labour market signals for these awards. Vocational qualifications currently play a marginal role in labour market recruitment and selection (Keep 2005a). The fact that the relatively new SSCs, whose ability to represent employers is in any case questionable (SSDA 2006), have been involved in determining the content of these new qualifications, is not guaranteed to make them the basis of recruitment by employers as whole.

Diplomas and inclusion

From the quotations cited earlier, it is clear that one of the roles that ministers and officials have seen the Diplomas playing is as motivational awards for disaffected young people. However, there are problems too with this particular purpose. Because the Government did not follow Tomlinson's advice to create a fully inclusive diploma framework from Entry Level upwards, it confined the Diplomas to Levels 1–3 only. This immediately excludes a significant minority of 14–19 learners who are unable to achieve full Level 1 awards or GCSE equivalents or who may not be attracted by the Diplomas' particular blend of theoretical and applied learning. This issue was raised in our interviews:

> So the Government's done one thing, which is to try to find a middle path with the Diplomas but actually it is, as it stands at the moment, still failing to address the needs of that rump of young people who are in the Ds and Es at GCSE, and for whom school has never really been a satisfactory experience. (PA 14)

As we have seen in Chapter 3, it is intended that these learners will be served by the Foundation Learning Tier (FLT), but the connections between the FLT and the Diploma system are less than clear, with the result that many young people could be excluded from established routes of progression through 14–19 education and training. Furthermore, the rejection of Tomlinson's concept of interlocking diplomas that comprise a mix of levels to aid progression and motivation may mean that learners are labelled by their Diploma level, which may prove a particular problem at Level 1. Not only are the Diplomas unlikely to achieve parity of esteem or fulfil a strong vocational role, they also appear to exclude more marginalized learners.

Who will take the Diplomas?

A big question arises, therefore, as to which groups of learners will choose, or be selected for, the Diplomas in an education market actively promoted by government. Historical precedent suggests that the retention of GCSEs and A Levels, which have been accepted as the most prestigious route of study for 14–19-year-olds for many years, will mean that the most able learners (and their parents) are likely to continue to opt for these qualifications rather than to choose one of the Diplomas. Universities' traditional preference for A Levels, and even the International Baccalaureate, will confirm this choice. Moreover, if Diplomas co-exist with tried and tested vocational qualifications, such as BTEC National Diplomas, CGLI and OCR awards, their popularity is not assured even amongst those learners wishing to take more applied or vocational study. There is, therefore, the danger of a repetition of the GNVQ and AVCE experience of a relatively low-status and low-profile award which has to compete with other more tried and tested qualifications. It may only be partially accepted by higher education and by employers, thus reducing both learner and end-user demand. One interviewee sounded a sceptical note: 'So I am intrigued as to who will take this brave new diploma ... I can't see that the things are in place for the Diploma to have this high bright sparkly profile' (PA 22). This person went on to say, 'I think it will be better when the secondary curriculum review comes up with similar packages for everybody, so the Diploma isn't seen as exceptional' (PA 22).

A 2007 survey of teachers' and further education lecturers' views about the Diplomas (Edge 2007) supported this analysis. While 57 per cent of respondents thought that Diplomas were potentially a good idea, 73 per cent did not believe that they would succeed in offering students a genuinely high-quality alternative to GCSEs and A Levels, and 90 per cent were convinced that the diplomas would not appeal to students from a middle-class background. Moreover, the majority of lecturers and teachers believed that parents, learners, universities and even teachers themselves would see Diplomas as having lower status than A Levels and GCSEs. The National Audit Office (2007) confirmed the problems facing the Diplomas from the perspective of educational professionals. They found that many were enthusiastic about the Diplomas approach to learning, but awareness amongst front-line staff was low and there were concerns about funding and the credibility of the new qualifications. A survey carried out at the end of 2007 by ICM, involving 803 headteachers, confirmed a lack of understanding of the new award, with 93 per cent highlighting the lack of parental and pupil knowledge of the new qualifications. This prompted the *Guardian* to declare that the Diplomas had got 'off to a halting start' (Shepherd 2008).

These factors and the perceptions they generate would appear to severely limit the role of the Diploma in the qualifications system as a whole. There are particular problems post-16 because of the dominance of established academic and vocational qualifications, as well as the attractions of Apprenticeships, which the Government is actively promoting (DIUS/DCSF 2008). The position is somewhat different, however, in relation to compulsory education because, arguably, there are fewer competitor qualifications for 14–16-year-olds and there has been a long-standing debate, going back to the 2002 14–19 Green Paper, about the need for more flexibility and vocational learning at Key Stage 4. Diplomas may, therefore, make a significant impact in the 14–16 curriculum, replacing GCSEs in vocational subjects and pre-16 GNVQs. In this location, the Level 1 and Level 2 Diplomas can be offered alongside a substantial number of GCSEs, forming a potentially attractive broad and balanced programme of study for younger learners. This curriculum model has been actively promoted by the 14–19 Pathfinders, and discussions with practitioners suggest that where the Diplomas may be most successful is in their role of enriching general education. However, even here there are problems with a middle-track award. The Diplomas neither offer the prestige of GCSEs, nor do they offer the sharply vocational focus of BTEC First Diplomas and other courses, which have been offered as part of the Increased Flexibility Programme (IFP).

Given these constraints, it is difficult to see how the Diplomas will play a bigger role in the 14–19 education and training system than any of their predecessor middle-track qualifications, despite the unprecedented amount of money, time and energy that has been invested in their development and marketing. In this context, the announcement in December 2007 that the UCAS tariff for the Level 3 Diploma will be equivalent to three-and a half A Levels, and that there will be an additional £1,000 available to schools and colleges for each student taking Diplomas (Lipsett 2007), might be seen as a deliberate policy to incentivize institutions to offer these awards. The risks are obvious. Institutions seeking league table points and funding may be tempted to advise learners to take Diplomas when they may not be suitable and when their recognition by end-users is still uncertain.

We now turn to the development process surrounding the Diplomas in order to discuss how problems of purpose and location are affecting design and implementation.

THE DESIGN PROCESS

As we will see, the main criticisms of the Diplomas have been directed at the design and implementation process (for example HoC 2007). We agree that there are significant problems associated with the development of the new qualifications, many of which stem from the political decision to design an entirely new award from scratch using an untried development process within a rushed timescale. However, we will also argue below that there is a direct relationship between all of these problems and the location of the Diploma as a middle-track qualification. The House of Commons Education and Skills Select Committee on 14–19 Diplomas' main anxiety was that because of the rushed and untried development process, the reputation of the Diplomas was being eroded even before they had been fully formed. Our criticism goes further. As we have argued earlier, history demonstrates that designing new middle-track awards is an extremely risky enterprise. Even if the implementation and design processes had been optimal, the award would still be facing difficulties because of its location in relation to established academic and vocational qualifications.

A new sequential approach to development

The DCSF hopes that the 'unique' design of the Diplomas will make them attractive to learners. Politicians and civil servants have made a virtue of Diplomas being designed in a completely new way in order to signify the novelty of the initiative.

The generic template for the Diplomas was primarily developed by private consultants working for the QCA, with very little time for full consultation either with qualifications experts or with practitioners. The designers attempted to incorporate some features of the Tomlinson proposals into the Diploma template (for example the Extended Project), but did not make significant use of existing vocational qualifications designs. This 'blank slate' approach was strongly criticized in the Select Committee Report because it was not convinced that the convergence between the Diplomas and other awards could simply be sorted out at a later stage. Many who gave evidence suggested that greater use should have been made of tried and tested qualifications such as BTEC awards (HoC 2007).

The DDPs, who were in charge of 'populating' the Principal Learning component, did not necessarily have the curriculum expertise required for this task. Furthermore, their credibility to represent the views of employers, particularly small and medium enterprises, was questioned by employer representatives giving evidence to the Select Committee (HoC 2007). It is difficult, therefore, to see how the Government's idea of involving employers in order to ensure their acceptance of the Diplomas is going to be served by this design process.

Meanwhile, awarding bodies, which did have the expertise to contribute to the Diplomas, were only allowed to play a marginal role in the initial design, even though they were later charged with developing the more detailed specifications, based on less than perfect content generated by the

DDPs. One awarding body claimed that 'most DDPs kept awarding bodies at arms length until they were close to completing their detailed Diploma content' (HoC 2007: 24). Although this was denied by the Secretary of State at the time, who claimed that the DDPs represented a wide range of stakeholders, the perception of an exclusive, new and risky approach to the design of the Diplomas persisted. The last stage in the design process was fulfilled by QCA. As the national regulator, it had overall say on the final designs and assessment.

What has occurred, therefore, is a sequential rather than a holistic approach to design, which has resulted in variability in content, the divorce of content and assessment, and the exclusion of expert inputs into the overall process, particularly in the early stages. The separation of roles for each of the three parties in the shaping of the Diplomas, particularly given the very short timescale for their development, has been fraught with communication problems. Moreover, this new and untried approach to qualifications design, in which bodies representing employment sector interests have been accorded the leading role, risks creating very different Diplomas in each of the 14 lines, which may restrict horizontal and vertical progression for learners within and across the framework. As Mike Tomlinson pointed out in his Final Report (Working Group on 14–19 Reform 2004a), this kind of learner mobility is particularly important at the lower levels of the new Diploma ladder because it is here that learners face the greatest barriers to progression under the current qualifications system. One interviewee summed up the sense of frustration:

> The first round of Diplomas was probably the most awful and awfully managed curriculum development I've ever had. It was unbelievable it was so bad, and most of us are still trying to recover from it. (PA 5)

There is some evidence that lessons have been learned and there is more openness, but this negative experience was unnecessary and damaged the development process.

The people who were excluded almost entirely from this design process were the practitioners, who have considerable experience of both curriculum development and teaching vocational qualifications. This exclusion, to which there were some notable exceptions, is problematic for at least two reasons: practitioners will ultimately be responsible for delivering the new awards and, therefore, need to be brought on board at an early stage; they also have the expertise to point out practical design faults that may otherwise go unnoticed until the implementation phase. The effects of a lack of practitioner involvement were succinctly summed up by Geoff Stanton in his evidence to the Select Committee: 'Firstly, it is wasteful to their potential contribution to the development process, secondly, it is highly likely that they will find themselves being asked to deliver qualifications that fail to provide a basis for the learning experiences that they would want for their learners and that the learners have been led to expect' (HoC 2007: 23). The NUT put it even more strongly:

> Teachers will be motivated to work towards a new system of Diplomas over a development period only if they are instrumental in developing curriculum models, modes of assessment and approaches to learning and teaching. The role of teachers has not been made explicit in the designing or delivery of the Diplomas. This will not inspire teachers' confidence to deliver imposed curriculum specifications/courses. (NUT 2007: 1)

Design and assessment issues

There are a number of other concrete issues that arise specifically from the design of the new awards.

Practitioners have pointed to the 'academic' approach that has been taken to the content of Principal Learning because of the lead role of the DDPs who were, as we have seen, increasingly concerned to chase parity of esteem. Because each of the DDPs took a different approach to Principal Learning, there is considerable variability in the content and focus in the first five Diploma lines. For example, construction and the built environment has a highly vocational and practical focus, while the engineering specifications make a virtue of their academic content, and creative and media Principal Learning demands engagement with a very broad range of vocational disciplines, ranging from fashion design to dance. Moreover, the DDPs took different approaches to the curriculum, with some ensuring that the same skills were revisited at each of the three levels, while others only introduced certain topics at a particular level. Although these variations could be regarded as a strength, because they reflect differences between the sectors, they also lead to questions of consistency, problems with progression between Diploma lines and, therefore, parity between different Diplomas in what is intended to be a single system.

As we have outlined in an earlier section, Diplomas have been designed as 14–19 awards. At Levels 1 and 2, they are supposed to meet the needs of 14–16-year-olds and 16–19-year-olds. Interestingly, the idea of a common template across the whole 14–19 phase was not something advocated by the

Tomlinson Committee. It suggested that up to the age of 16, only general diplomas would be offered to learners, although it was envisaged that these could contain sharply vocational and practical learning experiences. Specialized programmes of study would, therefore, only be undertaken post-16. A common template that covers the complete 14–19 phase has the potential to create problems for the award. Practitioners have highlighted the issue of learners pursuing vocational specialization pre-16. Learners of this age are not old enough to gain 'licence to practise' awards, such as those in childcare, so even if they pass a Level 2 qualification, they are not necessarily ready to go out into the workplace, unlike their post-16 counterparts. This raises a question about what the function of a sectoral vocational award, such as the Diploma, might be within compulsory education. In addition, if learners undertake sector-specific specialization pre-16, there is a danger of repetition of study post-16, particularly if they do not progress to the next level.

Assessment of the Diplomas is also causing consternation to both awarding bodies and practitioners. Due to the nature of Diplomas as a composite award, the assessment regime is viewed as complex because different components are assessed in different ways and have to be aggregated for the full award. There is concern about the amount of external assessment and the constrained nature of internal assessment, which appears to consist largely of timed tasks. An additional issue is how broader skills will be integrated within the Diplomas and the fact that Functional Skills will be assessed through written tests. Many of these assessment features appear to run counter to the applied or vocational nature of the award and have raised concerns about possible low pass rates, as well as validity. The fact that an overall Diploma grade will be determined by only Principal Learning and the Extended Project suggests that other components are considered as less important.

Equally complex is the whole awarding process for the Diplomas, with the possibility that learners will take individual components with different awarding bodies. Not only will this be difficult to track and record in order to accredit learners with the full Diploma, but it will also create considerable issues for quality assurance of the overall qualification.

IMPLEMENTATION

Tight time-scales – is the system prepared?

Problems of separating design functions and making the design process less than inclusive have been compounded by a rushed implementation timetable (HoC 2007). The original date for designing and piloting the first 14 Diploma lines was brought forward from 2013 to 2010, with the first five awards being delivered in September 2008 even before the full evaluation of some of its component parts (functional skills and the Extended Project) was complete. Moreover, as part of the Diploma Gateway Process announced in June 2006, which determined those consortia that would be allowed to pilot the first five lines of Diplomas, schools and colleges were having to make decisions about which Diploma lines to offer and even to indicate how many learners would take the new qualifications, prior to seeing the specifications for the new awards. This has meant that they have had to market the Diplomas to parents and learners without full knowledge of what they were and how they would be assessed and delivered.

One of the major concerns is about whether teachers and lecturers will be prepared to teach the Diplomas. Currently, priority has been given to those who are piloting the Diplomas in September 2008. Consortia have been offered three days of training by a range of national government agencies such as the Specialist Schools and Academies Trust and the Quality Improvement Agency. However, teacher and lecturer unions and professional associations have complained about the paucity of the training, the 'bunching' of reforms in 2008 and the lack of adequate time and resources for preparation (for example NUT 2007). Are the mistakes of *Curriculum 2000* being repeated?

Who will offer the Diplomas?

Institutional collaboration is seen as the key to the successful delivery of the Diplomas. As Chapter 6 will point out, however, collaborative arrangements between schools, colleges and work-based learning providers have been limited and fragile, a point made in the Select Committee Report (HoC 2007) and by LEACAN (Tirrell et al. 2006), an organization that represents local authority education advisers. What the latter report emphasizes is that local authorities, while having been given strategic responsibility for 14–19 learning since 2006, are often still finding their feet in this role. One interviewee articulated the reasons: 'I just fear that frankly the local authorities have not got the infrastructure to deal with 14–19, and particularly 16–19, because they stripped out all their FE people' (PA 17). Moreover, in London and other large metropolitan areas, a regional approach to organizing the 14–19 entitlement might be more appropriate (Grainger et al. 2007), but regions have not necessarily recognized this role nor have they been given the power to organize 14–19 learning.

In the meantime, it is clear from the *14–19 Implementation Plan* (DfES 2005b) that schools are expected to play a major role in delivering the Diplomas. It is unlikely, however, that they will be able to offer a large number because they will not have the facilities or specialist staff, despite the capacity-building measures described in the Plan. Colleges, on the other hand, while potentially the obvious providers of the vocational entitlement are, from discussions we have had with senior managers and sector representative bodies, concerned on at least four accounts about fulfilling this role. They are nervous of taking on new qualifications without a strong reputation. They are also concerned that some of the Diploma lines, at each of the levels, may attract very small numbers of learners and will make them costly to mount as courses. GNVQs taught FE colleges that some sector qualifications do not prove popular. In addition, colleges are anxious about the very broad nature of each of the original 14 lines and the risk of not being able to meet specific learner or employer needs without offering large numbers of costly specialised units. Furthermore, they are particularly concerned about the possibility that they will not receive adequate funding.

Finally, both schools and colleges are worried about the amount of employer engagement required to cover all the work-based elements at all levels of the new awards. This would demand a significant rise in the number of work experience placements available to 14–19-year-olds.

CONCLUSION – HELPING DIPLOMAS ESCAPE THEIR MIDDLE-TRACK TRAP

The evidence to date suggests that almost everyone involved in the reform process regards the Diplomas as problematical, but beyond this opinions diverge. The Government remains resolute in its determination to introduce these new awards, although they have vacillated between hype and panic. Diplomas are seen as an essential tool in raising the post-16 participation rate to 100 per cent through providing more choice for learners. For these reasons, as Lord Leitch stated, the Diplomas must succeed (Leitch 2006).

Critics, on the other hand, are equally resolute that the Diplomas, whatever their pedagogical merits, constitute an historic strategic error. They not only repeat the mistakes of the past as middle-track qualifications, but they also deflect resources and energy away from addressing deep-seated problems within the English education and training system which we associate, in particular, with the academic/vocational divide. The most harsh criticism has been reserved for Tony Blair's and Ruth Kelly's political decision to reject the main recommendations of the Tomlinson Report, which *The Independent* referred to as a 'spasm of political cowardice' (*Independent* 2007).

The Diplomas were born in an atmosphere in which 'Electoral Tactics have taken precedence over educational logic' (Dunford, cited in Curtis 2005).

There is a third position which accepts the Diplomas as a *fait accompli* and sees them as a bridgehead whereby the diploma concept gradually seeps into the academic track as part of a long and winding road to a more unified system. Practitioners, by the very nature of having to make provision work for learners, broadly occupy this third camp and could be referred to as 'pragmatic unifiers'. Their position has been reinforced by the recent decision to create three new general education Diploma lines.

Given this context, how should practitioners, researchers and policymakers respond to the Diplomas? In a recent Nuffield Review Issues Paper (2007) we argued the following. First, it is important that practitioners engage with the reforms to improve provision and progression for learners. Work by 14–19 Pathfinders suggests that the Diplomas will have a positive role to play at Levels 1 and 2 in Key Stage 4 as part of a strategy to broaden and modernize the upper secondary curriculum.[3] Second, the Government should learn from the problems associated with the design and implementation process to date. All partners, and particularly practitioners, who are responsible for making the reforms work, should be fully involved at all points in the reform process. Third, it should be recognized that BTEC awards and other existing vocational qualifications play a positive role, particularly post-16, and should be retained until Diplomas show that they can fulfil this function. Finally, the Government should now make it clear that A Levels and GCSEs will, over time, be subsumed within the Diploma framework, so that all 14–19-year-olds can benefit from broader programmes of study containing both theoretical and applied learning. If every young person took a diploma of one sort or another, then the diploma brand would be assured. This decision cannot be delayed until 2013 because, despite the announcement of the three new lines, all Diplomas will suffer in the shadow of A Levels.

NOTES

[1] The design features of the three new Diploma lines have not yet been decided.

[2] Since writing this chapter the Government has announced its intention to introduce Extended Diplomas at Levels 1, 2 and 3. These awards will be larger in volume than the existing 17 diploma lines.

[3] DfES 14–19 website on 14–19 Pathfinders, available at www.dfes.gov.uk/14-19/dsp_pfdetails.cfm, accessed 17 August 2007.

chapter 5

VOCATIONAL LEARNING, EMPLOYERS AND THE WORK-BASED ROUTE

THE ROLE OF VOCATIONAL LEARNING IN ENGLAND

In this chapter we examine vocational learning in the context of 14–19 education and training. We look at the relationship between general education, government funded vocational education in schools, colleges and private providers, as well as work-based programmes, with the exception of those for 16–19-year-olds in full-time paid employment. Stasz et al. (2004: 1) use the term 'vocational learning' to describe 'any form of activity and experiences leading to understandings or skills relevant to work' and we will work within this broad definition. However, in some parts of the chapter we need to make a distinction between vocational learning that takes place within educational institutions and provision which is substantially undertaken on employers' premises. The latter we refer to as the 'work-based route'.

There is an almost unanimous consensus that England should develop a larger and stronger work-based route for young people. However, its reality contrasts sharply with this shared vision. As we will see, it is poorly understood and very diverse in terms of programmes and experiences. Despite recent improvements in completion rates for apprenticeships and other vocational qualifications (LSC 2006a), its performance is still relatively poor both compared internationally and in relation to the academic track. This gap between desire and reality can be illustrated through the problems of policy-making in this area. Keep describes policy on the work-based route in England as a 'tethered beetle' (2005b) that constantly revisits old ideas and worn-out policy solutions, but never reaches its desired goal. This is an area of policy littered with good intentions and poor outcomes.

Since the late 1970s there have been numerous government schemes in the area of vocational education for young people, starting with Unified Vocational Preparation (UVP), the Youth Opportunities Programme (YOP) and the Youth Training Scheme (YTS). This was followed by the Technical and Vocational Education Initiative (TVEI) in the 1980s and early 1990s. More recently, initiatives have included Modern Apprenticeships (MAs), Young Apprenticeships (YAs), the Increased Flexibility Programme (IFP) and 14–19 Diplomas (see Stanton and Bailey 2004 for more detail).

Successive governments have seen vocational education, and the work-based route in particular, as a solution to two very different problems. The dominant policy approach, since the late 1970s and the collapse of a mass youth labour market, has been to use this area of education and training as a means of dealing with disaffection and as a second-chance route. The sub-ordinate aim has been to promote high-quality vocational education, signified by 'employer-led and employed status' apprenticeships.

In the final part of the chapter, we argue that these dominant and sub-ordinate approaches to vocational learning and the work-based route stem from the interaction of two fundamental factors. The first factor, as we saw in Chapter 3, is that general education is selective and aimed primarily at entry to higher education, with the result that the dominant image of voca-tional learning in the 14–19 phase is as a route for those who cannot succeed within this regime. Thus, vocational education in the school system is seen by young people and their parents as the lower-status option, an image which it never fully shakes off post-16, despite the existence of some high-quality and highly selective apprenticeships. Poor completion rates in vocational qualifications and apprenticeships and low rates of return in the labour market, when compared with academic qualifications, reinforce the low status of this pathway. This problem is further compounded by a stream of government initiatives, which confuses both employers and the general public about the nature and meaning of vocational education.

The second factor has its roots in the unregulated nature of the youth labour market in England (and in the UK more widely). Very few sectors operate strict 'licence to practise' policies and a tiny minority of employers offer apprenticeship places, both of which could serve to raise the status of vocational education. This also means that, in comparison with many other

European states, employers play a marginal role in the initial education of young people in this country. The void has to be filled by government initiatives involving FE colleges and independent training providers. The expansion of higher education since the late 1980s has further marginalized the work-based route, with Foundation Degrees now offering a substitute for higher level apprenticeships (Keep and Payne 2004).

THE VOLUNTARIST ENGLISH APPROACH

The English education and training system is broadly school- or college-based with low levels of employer engagement. FE colleges and independent learning providers play a major bridging role between education and work-based learning. As we have seen in earlier chapters, 14–19 learning in England is dominated by a full-time general education route, defined by A Level and GCSE courses. Other routes occupy a relatively minor position (see Figure 1.2).

More generally, recent economic and employment developments have served to frustrate the development of a more high-skilled work-based route in England. There are an increasing number of small- and medium-sized enterprises (SMEs), which are less likely to train than larger businesses (NAO 2005). This situation is compounded by poor levels of basic skills amongst some managers (Unwin and Ryan 2007) and the fact that many of these companies do not recruit below graduate level. Inward migration to the UK labour market is now also playing a major role in reducing the need for employers to offer training for young people. The rise in the number of skilled workers prepared to work for low wages, particularly from the new European accession countries, allows companies to address their skill shortages and reduces their need to train young people to fill a range of jobs in the future (LSC 2006b).

Unlike countries such as Germany and Switzerland, the UK does not have a strong history of social partnership between employers, trade unions, government and the education and training system, in which the different parties are bound by statutory agreement to regulate the youth labour market and to provide vocational learning (Hayward and James 2004). This has meant that the work-based route is reliant primarily on employer voluntary commitment to training, which is variable across sectors and depends very much on the size and historical traditions of particular companies. Engineering firms, for example, have a relatively good record, while retailing does not (Fuller and Unwin 2007). Sectors which have traditionally offered high-status apprenticeships tend to be in areas that employ male workers, with the result that there are fewer opportunities for young women. Moreover, many of the apprenticeships which attract female trainees appear to reinforce gender stereotyping (Colley 2006). Interestingly, the public sector is a poor performer when it comes to training young people and providing apprenticeship places (Nuffield 14–19 Review 2008a).

In this voluntarist context, government programmes, targets and exhortations have substituted for a strong social partnership approach (Stasz et al. 2004) and ironically take funding and powers away from employers (Ashton 2006). Others argue that employers are content to play a relatively passive consumer role in initial vocational education and training (Gleeson and Keep 2004). On the positive side, compared with other European countries, the English system might be viewed as flexible and responsive. As we will see, there is a myriad of programmes and courses tailored to the perceived needs of different groups of learners, giving rise to a complex system which allows young people a 'second chance' at the end of compulsory schooling. However, as we also discuss below, the penalty is often low-status, low-quality and fragmented provision.

VOCATIONAL LEARNING FOR 14–19-YEAR-OLDS

14–16 vocational learning

Vocational learning for 14–19-year-olds is overwhelmingly driven by government policy. During its first term of office (1997–2001), New Labour focused on *Curriculum 2000* for advanced level learners in full-time post-16 study, the New Deal for 18–24-year-olds and the continuation of Modern Apprenticeships for 16–25-year-olds (Hodgson and Spours 1999). It was only in 2002, with the publication of the 14–19 Green Paper (DfES 2002), that attention swung to Key Stage 4 and the promotion of vocational learning in compulsory education as a means of motivating young people and providing a progression route to further work-based learning post-16 (for example apprenticeships). Since 2004, there has also been a statutory entitlement to work-related learning (WRL) for all 14–16-year-olds. WRL is defined by the QCA as 'planned activity that uses the context of work to develop knowledge, skills and understanding useful in work' (QCA 2007d: 2). It is the responsibility of each school to determine its provision having regard to QCA guidance. While the QCA states that this work-related entitlement is having some effect on learning in Key Stage 4, the image of vocational learning as a whole is largely shaped by government initiatives for those alienated by or not deemed suitable for general education. Since 2002, the Government has encouraged schools to use a wide range of alternatives to traditional GCSEs, including GCSEs in vocational subjects, General National Vocational Qualifications (GNVQs), National Vocational Qualifications (NVQs), BTEC First Diplomas, the ASDAN Certificate of Personal Effectiveness (COPE) award and the BTEC Explorer, which now occupy a part of a 14–16-year-old learner's timetable.

The two common features of these qualifications are that they focus on the application of knowledge and that they rely less on assessment through examination than traditional GCSEs. This development has been supported largely through the government sponsored Increased Flexibility Programme (IFP), which has not only provided resources for schools to develop these alternatives, but has also encouraged collaboration between providers in a local area to offer study off-site for one or two days per week (see Golden et al. 2005). In 2006, approximately 90,000 pupils from 2,000 schools were involved (Teachernet 2007a). More recently, from 2004, provision at Key Stage 4 has been supplemented by Young Apprenticeships that share many of the characteristics of IFP but are sector-based and intended to provide a foundation for post-16 apprenticeships amongst the 'motivated and able'. In 2006, 3,500 young people started Young Apprenticeships in a range of sectors from art and design to food and drink manufacturing, science and the electricity industry (Teachernet 2007b).

In compulsory education, vocational learning operates, therefore, mainly as an alternative options programme to a full suite of nine or 10 GCSEs. It is thus experienced by a minority of 14–16-year-olds, usually for one or two days in the learning week (Golden et al. 2004). A recent evaluation report (Haines 2006) found that in many schools the less able, disaffected and disengaged learners were being targeted for NVQs and, to a lesser extent, applied GCSEs, even though their headteachers claimed that these options were open to a wider range of pupils. Moreover, students in disadvantaged areas were more likely to find themselves on NVQ programmes. This finding resonates with the Ofsted investigation into the applied GCSEs, which stated that 'in some schools the target group for the new courses is mainly lower attaining pupils' (Ofsted 2004: 3).

Nevertheless, these new work-related courses and experiences for 14–16-year-olds have proved very popular with those learners who have experienced them (for example Ofsted 2005; Golden et al. 2005; Steer and Grainger 2007). In the Steer and Grainger study, which examined the impact of a locally devised 'Raising Enjoyment and Achievement Programme' in Wolverhampton, learners stated that they had experienced a wide range of activities, many of which took place outside the school context. For the most part, the activities had a clear purpose and focus, learning was at the right pace, they were given regular feedback on their progress and they benefited from considerable individual attention. While these positive features may have derived from their 'vocational' context, they also appear remarkably like features of good general pedagogy.

It is less obvious to what extent these new programmes in Key Stage 4 have broadened the 14–16 curriculum for all learners, although a recent evaluation undertaken for QCA claims that, as a result of the work-related entitlement from 2004, there has been 'an increase in the provision that schools make for all their students. Enterprise activity has seen the largest increase' (QCA 2007d: 1).

Post-16 vocational learning

Post-16, full-time vocational learning becomes both more specialized and more diverse, with most programmes being offered within further educa- tion (FE) colleges, although a minority of school sixth forms offer a very small number of more generic or 'weakly vocational' courses. A typical col- lege prospectus, on the other hand, will contain a large number of courses for 14–19-year-olds at all levels from Entry to Level 3, but the nature of the provision will differ markedly depending on the institutional mix, compe- tition between providers, the make-up of communities, the labour market and travel-to-learn patterns in the locality, or what we refer to as the 'local ecology' (Spours et al. 2007a).

The majority of 16–19-year-olds not studying A Levels, therefore, find themselves choosing from a bewildering array of full-time college courses, many of which fit into what we described in the previous chapter as the 'middle track'. These programmes are normally of one or two years' duration (one year for Entry, Level 1 and Level 2, and two years for Level 3). Typically full-time learners will attend college for anything between 15–20 hours per week. The majority of programmes lead to a nationally- recognized qualification. Some colleges also provide locally tailored courses at Entry, Level 1 and Level 2, which comprise a package of nationally recognized qualifications that acts as a 'progression bridge' between qualification levels. Many of these programmes cater for learners with basic skills or English for Speakers of Other Languages (ESOL) needs. While these latter courses are taken by a small proportion of post-16 learners nationally, they constitute a large proportion of the provision in many inner-city areas and provide an important way of ensuring that young people remain within education and training until the age of 18 or 19. In addition, the Entry to Employment (E2E) Programme has been offered since 2003 for 16–18-year-olds 'who are not yet ready or able to directly enter apprenticeship programmes, further education or employment' (LSC 2006c).

Many of the courses offered within FE colleges require a certain amount of learning to be undertaken in a relevant workplace, although this will vary according to the qualification and, in many cases, will be confined to a short two- or three-week block of work experience. There are a range of college programmes, which sit between full-time education and the work-based route (for example hairdressing and plumbing), but these are in a minority in most FE colleges. Most of the teaching on vocational programmes will be undertaken by lecturers in dedicated facilities on the college site rather than by employers in a workplace. Furthermore, the success of these various full-time vocational learning programmes is primarily judged by learner achievement and completion rates and, to a lesser extent, by the numbers progressing to higher study. Government performance measures do not concentrate on progression into employment, even though these courses are ostensibly set up to prepare young people for work. In fact, the way that colleges are funded actually penalizes them if young people gain employment while they are studying and do not complete their qualification.

APPRENTICESHIP AND THE WORK-BASED ROUTE

Apprenticeship is the most publicly recognized aspect of the 'work-based route' in England. Since 2004, however, the 'apprenticeship' brand has been used for a range of vocational learning opportunities from Young Apprenticeships pre-16 to E2E, Apprenticeships and Advanced Apprenticeships post-16. As we have seen, the first two of these are, in fact, pre-vocational programmes. Apprenticeships (Level 2) and Advanced Apprenticeships (Level 3) in all sectors comprise a framework containing a national vocational qualification at the appropriate level and a Key Skills Qualification in communication, application of number and IT. Beyond this, it will be up to the individual sector skills council (SSC) responsible for that area of apprenticeship to decide on other requirements. Britain, unlike many other countries, has no statutory definition of apprenticeship (Ryan et al. 2006).

Apprenticeship and Advanced Apprenticeship programmes are now offered in three modes: (i) employer-led employed status; (ii) employer-led non-employed status programme-led; and (iii) programme-led in FE colleges (PLA). In the first case, the employer directly employs and pays the wages of the apprentice who has the opportunity to complete the qualifications necessary for the apprenticeship. In the second, the apprentice is registered as following a course with an employer or independent training provider leading to an apprenticeship, but does not have employed status. In the third type, based in an FE college, the young person is pursuing the qualifications that are part of an apprenticeship framework but without an employer placement. Fuller and Unwin make the point that 'this type of PLA falls well short of "guaranteeing" the sort of employer-based training that has been synonymous with apprenticeship' (2007: 8). Moreover, as they go on to state, it is quite possible to complete the qualifications but to be unable to find an employer to complete the apprenticeship. Thus, the term 'apprenticeship' is used by the Government to describe a variety of vocational programmes in schools, colleges and workplaces, many of which would not be recognized as such either internationally or even by the general public in England.

However, in 2008, the Government published a new strategy for England in which it proposed to 'strengthen' apprenticeships by a range of measures including: defining the meaning of apprenticeship more closely; increasing quality through a revised 'blueprint'; and specifying 'the accept-able minimum level of tie-in with employers' (DIUS/DCSF 2008: 6). The document states that apprenticeship, defined in this way, will be a route involving one in five of all young people in the next decade. Only time will tell whether these proposals will reverse the trend of what Government itself described as a 'severe decline in apprenticeships' (2008: 3).

In the meantime, the numbers of young people undertaking appren-ticeships is both small and declining, particularly at Level 3. A recent Nuffield Issues Paper, *Apprenticeship: Prospects for Growth* (Nuffield 14–19 Review 2008a), illustrates this pattern by showing participation in appren-ticeship measured in two ways: 'starts' (see Figure 5.1) and 'stocks' (see Figure 5.2).

What Figure 5.1 demonstrates is that the numbers commencing advanced apprenticeships have broadly remained static between 50,000 and 57,000 annually between 2001/2 and 2006/7. Starts of apprentice-ships at Level 2 during this period have always exceeded numbers at Level 3, peaking at 136,000 in 2003/4 but declining to 127,000 in 2006/7. While the numbers of people of all ages embarking on apprenticeships have fluctuated over the period 2000–2006, the overall picture of those entering the routeway is of a broadly static situation.

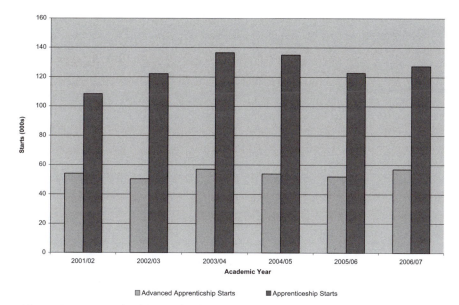

Figure 5.1 *Apprenticeships and Advanced Apprenticeships starts 2001/2–2006/7*
Source: Apprenticeship: Prospects for Growth (Nuffield 14–19 Review 2008a)

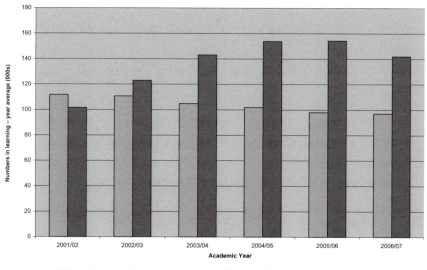

Figure 5.2 *Apprenticeships and Advanced Apprenticeships in learning 2001/2–2006/7*
Source: Apprenticeship: Prospects for Growth (Nuffield 14–19 Review 2008a)

Figure 5.2 shows that the number of participants in Apprenticeships rose steadily between 2000/1 to 2005/6 to 154,000, but has fallen back since to 142,000. Numbers participating in Advanced Apprenticeships have, on the other hand, declined steadily from 111,000 in 2001/2 to 97,000 in 2006/7. While overall numbers participating in the work-based route might look quite substantial, another picture emerges when they are examined through the lens of DfES participation statistics (DfES 2007a). In 2006, Advanced Apprenticeships accounted for only 1.7 per cent of 16–18-year-olds and Apprenticeships for 4.3 per cent.

In order to gain a representative picture of apprenticeship in England, these statistics about overall numbers need to be supplemented by more detailed information about sectoral differences. Apprenticeship frameworks are available in over 90 occupational sectors, although the vast majority of apprentices are found within 12, with the largest numbers involved in engineering, construction and hairdressing (Fuller and Unwin 2007).

Apprenticeship thus accounts for a small and declining part of the 14–19 education and training system. But the fact remains that apprenticeships are popular with some young people and their parents because they deliver favourable wage returns (McIntosh 2007) and, in some sectors, for example engineering, electrical trades and plumbing, apprenticeships still conjure up the image of skilled and respected work.

At this point, therefore, it is fair to ask why, if a stronger work-based route enjoys widespread political support and a proportion of young people wish to follow it, it has not grown and why does it still play a minor role in the English education and training system? In what follows, we identify three inter-related factors that we suggest trap vocational learning and the work-based route in a low-status, low-visibility, low-supply syndrome.

THREE DEEP-ROOTED ISSUES

Vocational learning, inclusion and academic drift

The status of vocational learning in the English system appears to be determined by the dominant role of selective academic education, the reactive role of vocational education and weak employer engagement. Taken together, these three factors lead to what has been termed 'academic drift' (see Table 3.1).

From the perspective of the whole 14–19 phase, as we have seen earlier, vocational learning is overwhelmingly associated with schools up to the age of 16 and then with FE colleges. Very little government-funded provision takes place on employer premises. The work-based route thus plays a relatively minor role and within this, high-status apprenticeships constitute a tiny part of the landscape. Moreover, what takes place in Key Stage 4 in the name of vocational education could more accurately be seen as pre-vocational, applied and practical. Even post-16, many of the courses in colleges could not be viewed as 'strongly vocational' (Stanton 2004). Some so-called vocational qualifications do not even have work experience as a requirement of successful completion. While the majority of these qualifications lead to higher study, with the possible exception of some BTEC and City and Guilds awards, they are not well recognized by employers, do not feature strongly in recruitment and selection processes and do not produce high rates of return for learners when compared with their academic counterparts (Keep 2005a). This argument was confirmed by one our interviewees who has an intimate knowledge of the employer landscape:

> *Any vocational qualification offer, or applied qualification offer, that there's been in the past has always sort of struggled because employers haven't really got to grips with it or understood it well enough to actually ask for it for their company. (PA 2)*

This is not helped by the confusion and disagreement about the definition of vocational education. The term 'vocational' is used loosely to signal to young people that their educational experiences will be different from general education, as defined by GCSEs and A Levels. So, from the beginning of the 14–19 phase, what is termed 'vocational education' is being shaped by the dominant academic qualification track rather by the demands of its own purposes, values and pedagogy. In effect, it is a residual category, defined by what it is not. Several interviewees referred to the shaping role of academic education. One pointed to the way in which broad vocational qualifications gravitate towards general education: 'Every other development has started off filling a space, the vocational space, and then has moved across and it's academic drift every time' (PA 9), while another talked about the need for 'an academic glaze applied to any kind of learning to make it acceptable and rigorous' (PA 14). The QCA and the Diploma DDPs are so sensitive about this issue that the term 'vocational' has been effectively banned.

There is, therefore, a strong argument for reserving the term 'vocational' for describing qualifications and programmes that have an intimate connection with the workplace and prepare and qualify young people for the labour market. This more focused concept would also sit comfortably with a more rationed approach to apprenticeship, reserving the term for employer-led and employed-status programmes. We return to this argument at the end of the chapter as we discuss the development of work-based learning within a social partnership framework.

The overall thrust of government policy on vocational learning and the work-based route in 14–19 education and training, particularly since 2002, has taken a very different direction. Its major aim has been to increase the number of alternative experiences and programmes available to young people as part of a 'choice' agenda and as a pragmatic response to learner disaffection. Vocational learning has been seen by government as motivational (DfES 2005a). It might thus be viewed as a strategy of inclusion intended to offset the negative effects of the academic track and to keep young people engaged with some form of education and training until the age of 18.

This pragmatic approach has experienced its successes, including high learner satisfaction rates (LSC 2006d) and an increase of 1 per cent in initial progression into post-compulsory education and training at 16 from 88.7 per cent in 2005 to 89.7 per cent in 2006 (DfES 2007a). However, the introduction of new 'vocational' qualifications at Key Stage 4 since 2002 appears to have boosted participation in full-time education and training post-16 rather than increasing the numbers in work-based learning (Hayward et al. 2006). Moreover, despite short-term performance gains, the overall effect of the 'inclusion approach' has been to perpetuate the low-status image of vocational learning (Fuller 2004). The sheer diversity of programmes and initiatives appears to lower its public visibility. Following the alternative and inclusion image of vocational learning in Key Stage 4, post-16 E2E courses, vocational qualifications below Level 3 and even Level 2 Apprenticeships continue to be associated with under-achievers. Status is only to be found in some Level 3 vocational qualifications such as BTEC National Diplomas. Advanced Apprenticeships too are very much sought after (Nuffield Review 2008a) but, as we have seen, involve a very small percentage of 14–19-year-olds and of these, very few indeed are employer-led with employment status. High-quality and high-visibility vocational and work-based learning simply drowns in a sea of disparate, low-status remedial provision in which the concept of vocational becomes diluted beyond recognition.

Variable quality

The problems of low status and dilution have been exacerbated by variable quality in vocational and work-based learning (Nuffield 14–19 Review 2008b). Problems of quality find many reflections. First, there is the variability of training traditions and training requirements across different employment sectors (Fuller and Unwin 2003). Within the UK, there are 300 separate apprenticeship frameworks, of which only a few (for example engineering and electro-technical occupations) have a strong impetus to train to Level 3 (Fuller and Unwin 2007). The House of Lords Report on *Apprenticeship* (House of Lords 2007) commented that apprentices on engineering and electro-technical occupations also have more opportunities to engage in off-the-job training to achieve recognized qualifications such as BTEC National Diplomas than in other sectors such as retailing.

The nature of the labour market plays a strong role in the size and quality of vocational education and training. As Keep and Mayhew point out, much employment in England does not demand high skill:

> Far from seeking an autonomous workforce of polyvalent knowledge workers to whom high levels of discretion have been delegated in order to produce high-spec, customized goods and services, many organizations continue to need workers to perform narrowly specified, closely supervised, repetitive tasks, in an environment where the work has been organized and the job designed in order to allow minimal discretion. (1998: 11)

Reflecting this picture of the labour market, frameworks in certain sectors focus their efforts on Level 2 or below. The pattern of skill demand is becoming increasingly polarized (Lauder 2001) and restricts the demand by employers for Level 3 apprenticeships (Brown et al. 2001). Hence the lower numbers of Advanced Apprenticeships when compared with Apprenticeships at Level 2 and the fact that demand for apprenticeships by young people outstrips supply (Nuffield 14–19 Review 2008a).

The problem of quality has been reflected in inspection reports on work-based learning (for example ALI 2006), with lower completion rates in vocational courses and in apprenticeships than in general education (Hayward et al. 2005). Here there have been improvements in recent years with many of the less effective independent learning providers being forced to go out of business, to merge or to move into other markets. Success rates for LSC-funded provision for 16–18-year-olds in further education has improved from 64 per cent in 2001/2 to 75 per cent in 2005/6, and completion rates for apprenticeships have doubled from 27 to 54 per cent over the same period (LSC 2007). However, the rate of improvement is variable across different sectors and is low in comparison with completion rates in countries with established apprenticeship systems, for example 79 per cent in Germany (Hayes and Kelly 2007). Moreover, the internal education demands of apprenticeships have become more permissive: it is no longer necessary to gain a technical certificate to complete an apprenticeship, and some on-the-job requirements have been reduced (Fuller and Unwin 2007).

The general education content of apprenticeship frameworks in England has traditionally been much weaker than in other European countries (Green 1998) and is becoming more so. Within this overall picture, there are sharp contrasts between good and not-so-good practice. This has been highlighted by research into 'restrictive' and 'expansive' work-based learning environments (Fuller and Unwin 2003).

In compulsory and full-time education and training, problems of quality within vocational and work-related learning courses take a somewhat different complexion. Here the issue is often the lack of a genuine work-based context in which to undertake learning and to contextualize the skill and knowledge demands of the qualification. So-called vocational qualifications in schools are still delivered primarily in the classroom by teachers who have little or no experience of the workplace about which they are teaching, nor do they always have the specialist facilities required to practise the skills associated with these qualifications (Ofsted 2007). Colleges have more facilities and specialist staff and the Centres of Vocational Excellence initiative has sought to improve their capacity in this respect. However, as Billett (2004) argues, there is no substitute for the workplace with its technical and human demands and pedagogic possibilities.

Quality in vocational learning is not helped by funding inequalities between schools, colleges and work-based learning providers, with the former receiving more advantageous resources than the latter two (Coffield et al. 2008). Moreover, Level 3 courses are more generously funded than lower-level courses (Stanton and Fletcher 2006), even though the latter are expected to remediate for poor attainment in school.

Employers, employment and government strategy

At the heart of the problem of vocational learning and the work-based route lies the issue of employer engagement and the nature of employment in modern Britain. First and foremost, there is no strong tradition of a social partnership approach to vocational education and training, such as that which exists in the Nordic countries, Germany and Austria and even Ireland (Boyd 2002). Social partnership ensures that a range of voices from employers, trade unions, the community, education and training specialists and government shape policy and practice. This can lead to a better relationship between skill demand and the supply of education and training, both of which are collectively determined. Steedman (2001) suggests that those countries with more established social partnership arrangements are able to produce a higher quality apprenticeship system than in the UK.

Even though the benefits of social partnership for vocational education and training are well documented in international comparative research, this is not an approach that English policy-makers have been prepared to take. Instead a voluntarist paradigm prevails (Hayward and James 2004). Voluntarist assumptions mean that the issue of employer engagement is discussed primarily in terms of business advantage and the cost to the employer of involvement in education and training, although use is also made of exhortation for employers to play their part in up-skilling the nation (for example Leitch 2006). In the absence of a common social partnership arrangement, policy has had to privilege the employer voice, using terms such as 'employer-led', in order to encourage their participation, although employers themselves would dispute the fact that they lead current government policy (CBI 2007). Moreover, a recent survey undertaken for the Sector Skills Development Agency (SSDA) suggests that so-called employer bodies, such as the SSCs, do not directly represent the voice of employers (SSDA 2006). The result is that many employers do not feel that current government sponsored education and training programmes meet their needs (NAO 2005). In this voluntarist climate, where it has proved difficult to stimulate employer engagement, a range of government-sponsored agencies act as intermediaries in the organization of work-based learning (Hayes and Kelly 2007). They invest considerable effort in identifying the training needs of regions, sectors and individual employers and in offering advice on training needs analysis (NAO 2005).

Government policy for 14–19 education and training as a whole calls for much greater employer engagement with all types of work-related and vocational qualifications, as well as with apprenticeships. The increase in the numbers of these programmes, as part of the choice and inclusion agenda, confronts employers with a bewildering array of roles and tasks (Huddleston et al. 2005) that they cannot possibly deliver. One of our interviewees, a leading employer, commented:

> There is a very clear list of requirements of employers to implement not just the Diplomas but policy ... and it's a long list. I mean it's not just work experience for diplomas, it's employment for apprentices, it's not just input into the qualifications structure, it's participating in the boards of schools and colleges, it's just a long list. (PA 8)

The main effort by government in the area of apprenticeship, for example, has therefore been to stimulate the supply of places by setting challenging targets for the LSC and creating brokerage arrangements between employers and government agencies. This substitutes for genuine signalling from employers about the needs of their sector (Hayes and Kelly 2007). In addition, the Government uses programmes such as *Train to Gain*, which offers financial incentives for training, together with weak regulatory arrangements (for example the statutory right to paid time off work to study for 16–17-year-olds not qualified to Level 2, the Disability Discrimination Act and licence to practice in a small minority of sectors), to increase employer involvement in education and training. This 'supply-led' approach, despite all the rhetoric about employer-led policies, forces employers into a passive role (Fuller and Unwin 2003). While it is maintained that employers spend £23 billion on training, and the CBI (2007) reported that this figure had risen to £33 billion, much of this is accounted for by management time, training costs and trainee wages within enterprises (NAO 2005). Involvement in public education and training by both the private and public sectors is low. For example, only 5 per cent of employers, mainly very large companies, contract with the LSC to run apprenticeships, although others will organize these through training providers (Fuller and Unwin 2007).

The void created by 'the curious absence of employers' from 14–19 education and training (Keep 2005a) leads to FE colleges, independent training providers and the voluntary sector substituting for their presence. However, as we have seen, these environments neither provide a direct experience of a workplace, with all the pedagogic and personal development advantages that this brings, nor can they ensure that the qualifications they offer will lead to secure and well-paid employment. The plethora of substituting organizations and intermediaries make the voluntarist environment a complex one, with the possibility that such a cluttered landscape might actually make engagement more difficult. The National Audit Office (2005) suggests that employers are confused by the number of different agencies with whom they have to liaise and that these agencies' bureaucratic requirements absorb unnecessary amounts of time. In addition, many small- and medium-sized companies require business support rather than skills brokerage to build their capacity to take on apprentices and to become involved in training (Fuller and Unwin 2007).

CONCLUSION – VOCATIONAL LEARNING AS PART OF A UNIFIED 14–19 PHASE

Despite constant policy intervention by successive governments over the last 30 years, vocational learning and the work-based route are still struggling with issues of status, size, quality and role. In 2007, it is possible to argue that they are caught in a low-supply, low-status, low-visibility and low-quality syndrome.

Most academics who write about this area understandably focus on the history of vocational education, the relationship between the labour market and vocational learning and the characteristics of the work-based route, assessing government policy in the light of this perspective. Here, while drawing heavily on their work, we examine vocational learning through the lens of 14–19 education as a whole. This perspective leads to similar but additional suggestions for reform to create a new settlement in which vocational learning and the work-based route play a larger and more high-status role within a more coherent 14–19 system.

We see little prospect of further improvements in participation and achievement in post-compulsory education without substantial growth in the work-based route at 16+ and an improvement in its status. This development we link to the future of general education as part of a more unified and inclusive 14–19 phase, as well as changes to policies on the labour market. It means viewing the problems of vocational education, in the first instance, as rooted in its negative relationship with the dominant academic track. Selective general education forces vocational education to play an inclusive and subordinate role. In fact, the recent Government proposals for 'strengthening' GCSEs and A Levels, discussed in Chapter 3, are likely to exacerbate the decanting of disaffected and lower-attaining learners into an alternative vocational pathway, particularly in the current policy context of 100 per cent participation up to the age of 18.

What we propose in this book (see Chapter 7) is a more open and inclusive approach to general education. It is important to offer all 14–19-year-olds different types of general education, including practical, applied, experiential and community-based learning, which will be motivational and which they can pursue beyond the age of 16 regardless of pace of progress. As a result, vocational education will be able to play its rightful role in relation to skill formation and employment. Furthermore, precious employer resources could be deployed higher up the system where they can be most effective. This proposal forms part of an argument that a more unified, rather than a more divided 14–19 system, will promote more strongly vocational education and training. However, it is not an argument that has been either properly understood or accepted by academics who specialize in the study of vocational education and training. They tend to see unification as promoting academic drift and encouraging dilution of vocational learning. We, on the other hand, associate these problems with the divided and weakly linked 14–19 system we currently possess.

Our second major conclusion, and one which chimes much more closely with academic colleagues in this area, is that we need a more regulatory and social partnership approach, with a more clearly defined role for all partners. Fuller and Unwin for example, assert that an effective and contemporary model of apprenticeship would involve 'the rebuilding of the relationship between community and apprenticeship within the framework of current economic, occupational and social conditions' (2003: 23). This suggests that we need to get away from seeing employers simply as what Macleod and Hughes (2005) refer to as 'stakeholders' or 'consumers' and to think of them more as 'strategic partners' in education and training. It is important to communicate that while employers are important partners, they are one of several. Within a broad social partnership agreement, it is possible that all partners would know more clearly where they stood and what was expected of them, rather than unrealistic expectations being made of any one partner.

So where is current government policy proceeding with regard to vocational learning and the work-based route? While it is difficult accurately to decode the thinking of the new Brown administration at this early stage, it appears that there is little significant change over the Blair years in terms of employment policy. The emphasis is still on voluntarism, with the Leitch agenda taking this to a new stage by promoting markets and privileging the voice of employers in the design of vocational qualifications through an enhanced role for SSCs. The Government seems more inclined towards organizational change than towards sharing power between the different social partners. The splitting of the education ministries, based on a 14–19 and adult skills divide, has left FE and apprenticeships in some sort of no-man's land. Despite mounting evidence that the voluntarist paradigm does not work effectively in promoting a high-status, high-volume and high-quality vocational learning and work-based route, it looks as if the 'tethered beetle' of skills policy is about to undertake yet one more turn.

chapter 6

14–19 ORGANIZATION AND GOVERNANCE: TOWARDS STRONGLY COLLABORATIVE SYSTEMS

THE INSTITUTIONAL LANDSCAPE IN ENGLAND

This chapter discusses government policy on organization and governance, characterizing the current institutional arrangements for 14–19 education and training as still strongly competitive and weakly collaborative. It describes the various types of partnership arrangements that have been formed as a result of recent government policies, identifies some of the drivers and inhibitors of their development and outlines the dimensions of a more strongly collaborative approach. The final part of the chapter focuses on wider governance issues resulting both from policy on devolution and from the needs of 14–19 education and training. It concludes by making the case for a shift in governance arrangements to move towards a more strongly collaborative learning system.

In a speech to the Fabian Society in November 2007, the Secretary of State for the Department for Children, Schools and Families (DCSF), Ed Balls, reiterated the Government's intention to raise the education participation age to 18 by 2015. He laid out four specific measures required to make this policy aspiration a reality: improved curriculum and qualifications; impartial advice and guidance for young people; financial support; and increased employer engagement with education and training (DCSF 2007a). He also announced a specific 'safety net' strategy to tackle the particular problems associated with the 10 per cent of young people not in any form of employment, education or training (NEET). Taken together these policies appear to constitute a well thought-out approach to what is an ambitious but necessary aim for both economic and social justice reasons, although this logic has been questioned (for example Wolf 2007).

What lies behind these measures, however, is a highly complex set of institutional, organizational and governance arrangements. Implementing the policy of raising the age of participation to 18 involves multiple national, regional and local government ministries and agencies, some directly under government control and others working in an arms-length manner, hundreds of different education and training providers, with different missions and conditions of employment for staff, serving different groups of learners and with varying degrees of autonomy from central or local government, as well as employers and other privately-owned partners who are expected to participate in a voluntary manner. It is this organizational and governance landscape in England which constitutes the subject of this chapter.

The New Labour Government can be seen to have pursued two separate and often conflicting policies on 14–19 organization and governance.[1] On the one hand, it has actively encouraged institutional diversity as part of its public service choice agenda and has asserted that competition between providers will drive up quality (PMSU 2006). The Government's priority has been to provide a choice of institutions and to bring more private capital into state education (Ball 2007). On the other hand, it has also pursued the idea of institutional collaboration to deliver the national 14–19 Entitlement (see Chapter 1) which, the Government argues, is best organized through schools, colleges and work-based learning providers working in partnership (DfES 2005a). The result of these two policies is an institutional framework that is complex and, more contentiously, is highly selective at the age of 16 (Stanton 2005).

England currently thus has a mixed economy of institutions delivering 14–19 education – there is no one organization that offers the whole range of provision for young people of this age. While most 14–19-year-olds still undertake the majority of their education in schools and colleges, as a result of the national 14–19 policies described in earlier chapters, a significant minority is now studying on employers' premises, with independent training providers or out in community settings. Even for those in full-time education, there is a wide choice of competing types of state schools and colleges with varied specialisms, admissions procedures, religious affiliations and governance arrangements, quite apart from the small but influential independent school sector. How much choice you have about where you study as a young person will also depend on which part of the country you happen to live in and what the organizational history in that area has been. At the same time, financial inducements, statute, curriculum pressure, targeted national initiatives and government exhortation are all being used to try to forge these various institutions into local partnerships to deliver the national 14–19 Entitlement and to encourage all young people to remain in education and training until the age of 18.

In terms of governance, schools and colleges have had a large degree of autonomy over their budgets since the 1988 Education Reform Act, which devolved more responsibilities to schools, and the 1992 Further and Higher Education Act, which gave Incorporation status to FE colleges. Independent learning providers, which have become increasingly important players in the provision of work-based and work-related areas of 14–19 education and training, vary considerably. Some are private for-profit organizations, others are charities catering for specific groups of learners and many operate in partnership with colleges or local authorities (LAs).

As individual institutions gained more powers to manage their own affairs from 1988 onwards, so the role of Local Education Authorities (LEAs) diminished. In the last two years, however, LAs, increasingly working through Children's Trusts, have become more central to policy for 14–19 education and training, having been given statutory responsibility for ensuring the delivery of the 14–19 Entitlement in their locality, as part of the *Every Child Matters* agenda (DCSF 2007g).[2] This was seen as a problem for 14–19 because, as one interviewee remarked:

> *They're (LAs) undergoing great changes at the moment into Children's Services and so what used to be a LEA with teams which had education as their centre, has now become part of a much larger structure and smaller units. 14–19 development has got lost in that change and what we're finding is that 14–19 teams are disappearing in terms of status and clout and you do have to have clout to bring about change. (PA 21)*

GOVERNMENT POLICY ON THE ORGANIZATION OF 14–19 EDUCATION AND TRAINING

While the raising of the participation age was only announced in 2007, in effect policy has been moving in this direction for several years. Government policy documents in this area, such as the 14–19 Implementation Plan, describe the 'new national curriculum and qualifications entitlement' for 14–19-year-olds as the 'centrepiece of our programme of reform' (DfES 2005b: Summary: para 4), going on to state that 'The entitlement that we propose could not be delivered by an individual school acting alone and nor could many colleges offer it' (2005b: para 10). The implication is that these organizations should work together to make the entitlement a reality for young people in each locality, although there will be 'no uniform, nationally-imposed model of delivery' (2005b: para 18). Instead, LAs have been given a statutory responsibility to ensure that all young people in their area have access to their entitlement. Moreover, since September 2007, LAs have had to take the lead strategic role in ensuring that the so-called 'September Guarantee' is delivered to all young people completing compulsory education in their area. This requires them to make sure all school-leavers receive the information, advice and guidance they need to apply for appropriate post-16 provision, that they have an offer of an appropriate place by the end of September of that year, monitoring those who do not and supporting them with their application, and to ensure that there is adequate provision in their area (DCSF 2007h).[3]

All of this appears to suggest the need for more local planning of provision or oversight of institutional arrangements within an area. However, other major policy texts on schools (for example DfES 2005c), colleges and work-based learning providers (DfES 2006e; DIUS 2007) stress instead the importance of institutional diversity and autonomy in terms of mission and governance, the need for 'contestability' and the market to drive up quality and the over-riding desire for a 'demand-led' rather than a planned system. These tensions between institutional competition and autonomy, on the one hand, and institutional collaboration and local planning on the other, are further complicated by the range of policy levers that national government uses in this area, some which support the former and some the latter.

POLICY LEVERS AND THEIR EFFECTS ON INSTITUTIONAL BEHAVIOUR

It is possible to identify five major national policy levers that affect the way that leaders and managers in schools, colleges and work-based learning make decisions about the provision of 14–19 education and training: performance tables/targets, inspection, funding, qualifications and policy initiatives. All of these are powerful in affecting institutional behaviour and the way providers relate to other institutions in their local area (Coffield et al. 2008).

Two of the policy levers – performance tables/targets and inspection – clearly support institutional autonomy rather than collaboration because they are focused primarily on the performance of the individual provider (for example the percentage of learners gaining 5 A*-C grades at GCSE) rather than on collective goals and outcomes (see Perry and Simpson 2006). Funding, 14–19 qualifications and policy initiatives, on the other hand, while still largely driving institutional competition, currently provide a mild stimulus to collaborative behaviour in the provision of 14–19 learning opportunities. However, vocational learning programmes are expensive in comparison with their general education counterparts and, according to a study by Styles and colleagues (2006), lack of funding is preventing many schools from collaborating with FE colleges and work-based learning providers to extend this kind of provision. Moreover, most funding is allocated according to the number of learners on roll, the qualifications they are taking and success rates – all of which encourage competitive behaviour. On the other hand, certain funding streams, such as those associated with delivery of the new 14–19 diplomas, come with conditions attached that emphasize collaborative behaviour. It is necessary, for example, to demonstrate strong partnership development in order to access any of the 'Diploma Gateway' funding (see Chapter 4).

In addition, some national 14–19 policy initiatives strongly privilege and support collaboration, but others make joint planning and organization of learning very difficult in a local area. In a recent study on inter-school collaboration, Atkinson and colleagues (2007) noted 17 different national government initiatives promoting partnership working between schools, the majority of which were open to providers of secondary education. 14–19 Pathfinders, for example, made collaboration a condition of funding.

In terms of the policy initiatives which make collaboration more difficult, perhaps the best example is the City Academies programme. Academies, which often replace failing schools in inner-city areas, are funded directly by central government and sponsored by business, faith or voluntary groups. They are not, therefore, under the jurisdiction of LAs. Until July 2007, they were not even required to follow the National Curriculum and were seen as wholly independent of other state schools in a locality. In most cases, they have acquired state-of-the-art accommodation and facilities and have been resourced more favourably than neighbouring schools and colleges. They have thus made the task of planning provision in a local area highly problematical for LAs and often disrupt 14–19 partnerships.

The struggle between collaboration and competition remains unequal. Reinforced by funding, performance and accountability steering mechanisms, the deeply embedded and historical set of competitive institutional arrangements too often overshadows the relatively weak, largely initiative-based policy levers for collaboration. Tensions in government policy were highlighted by an interviewee:

> *There is a real question about how the local needs are going to be met by the local partnerships because of the extraordinary disincentives that there are in schools to co-operate and to go into partnership ... and so you've got all sorts of legacy targets and policies, particularly league tables, which are driving all sorts of perverse behaviour on the part of schools, regardless of these new aspirations of government. (PA 14)*

14–19 COLLABORATIVE ARRANGEMENTS AND PARTNERSHIPS

Despite the dominance of competition and selection, many institutions recognize the benefits of collaboration, not only for their learners but also for their own viability. For 11–18 schools with small sixth forms, collaboration can provide economies of scale and greater choice. Schools catering for 11–16-year-olds benefit from collaboration because it allows them to provide a more motivational curriculum for 14–16-year-olds and clearer progression routes post-16, while for colleges and work-based learning providers collaboration with local schools potentially attracts more learners into post-16 study in their organizations.

Research evidence suggests that collaborative arrangements can:

- increase the range of provision for 14–19 learners at different levels (Principal Learning 2003; O'Donnell et al. 2006);
- open up new or enhanced progression routes and make them more transparent (DfES 2005a);
- extend advanced level choices and protect minority subjects (Hodgson and Spours, 2003); and
- enhance the quality of provision (Principal Learning 2003).

Much of the literature on collaboration focuses on the nature of partnerships and the structures needed to make collaborative arrangements work. Less detail is given about how partnership working affects learners. The more recent studies (for example Higham and Yeomans 2006; O'Donnell et al. 2006), however, suggest that collaborative arrangements are beginning to impact on provision for 14–16-year-olds as well as 16–19-year-olds, with a small number of partnerships reaching the stage of adopting arrangements for common timetabling, joint funding and quality assurance systems. These studies offer illuminative examples of collaboration, although it is difficult to quantify their extent on a national scale. What the studies do provide, however, is useful information on how various models of 14–19 collaboration are emerging to meet different local needs.

These models range from tightly managed, jointly-owned organizations through to looser and more occasional forms of collaboration for particular purposes. The common feature of all these models is their attempt to offset the negative effects of a predominantly competitive and divided system in order to meet the 'horizontal' and 'vertical' progression needs of particular groups of learners in a local area. Beyond this, there is a great deal of variation both in the learners they serve, the type of provision they offer, the degree of institutional autonomy and integration and their model of governance. Furthermore, many are currently sustained by short-term national funding related to particular initiatives.

The Nuffield Review of 14–19 Education and Training (Hayward et al. 2006) cited evidence from recent studies showing that collaborative arrangements between schools, colleges and, to a lesser extent, work-based learning providers are both expanding and deepening. Impetus has largely come from national government initiatives related to the 14–19 reform programme, such as the Increased Flexibility Programme (IFP), the 14–19 Implementation Plan and the Diploma Gateway process. In addition, there have been specific interventions by organizations such as the Learning and Skills Network, which has used government funding to support vocational learning and partnership development. By the end of the 14–19 Pathfinder programme in 2005, 39 areas across England had received considerable financial resources to test and pilot various aspects of 14–19 reform. The final evaluation report identified key legacies from this initiative in the Pathfinder areas (Higham and Yeomans 2006), including the development of substantial collaborative arrangements and leadership, the establishment of organizational structures to support collaboration and the development of staff with networking skills to facilitate partnership working.

In terms of institutional collaboration, a particular galvanizing moment was the publication of the first Diploma Gateway prospectus in 2006 (DfES 2006c). The most important criterion for selection to offer the Diplomas was evidence of collaborative working. Consortia were awarded a grade from 1–4 (with 4 being low) to indicate their state of readiness. Around half of the applications were graded 4, so it may be assumed that these partnerships were still in their infancy. The National Audit Office report (2007) confirmed this 'variable' state of readiness, with a third of all 14–19 consortia reporting that they were only in the early stages of implementing their 14–19 strategy. It also commented that employer engagement was the least developed aspect of most partnerships.

However, a small number of consortia, particularly in the Pathfinder areas (for example Wolverhampton, Kingswood, York, Cumbria and Gateshead), appear to have developed more advanced features, such as shared provision, common timetabling, joint funding, and quality assurance systems. Learning visits have been organized in an attempt to spread this good practice more widely. However, conditions for collaborative working vary in different parts of the country due to the influence of the historical legacy of institutional arrangements or geography and having to operate without the additional funding that was given to the 14–19 Pathfinders. Moreover, as NAO reported in 2007, the focus of funding on more developed partnerships that were successful in the Diploma Gateway risks leaving less successful partnerships behind.

FACTORS DRIVING AND INHIBITING PARTNERSHIP

While there is no absence of literature advising on the factors that support collaborative working (see Figure 6.1), not all of these factors are within the control of the institutions themselves. Even where they are, there are particular difficulties with 14–19 partnerships because of the varied nature of the institutions which need to be brought together to offer the full range of provision. The aims and values of an 11–16 comprehensive school, which has no provision for 16–19-year-olds, for example, is likely to be quite different from those of an 11–18 faith school or a City Academy wishing to build up numbers in its sixth form. The priorities of a sixth form or general FE college will be different again, and will certainly not be the same as those of a privately owned training provider or employer.

In addition, studies on 14–19 partnership working suggest that there is a formidable list of factors that are likely to inhibit collaboration (see Figure 6.2), some of which are practical (for example common timetabling, transport) and others of which are cultural and structural (for example institutional competition). The former, while difficult to resolve, are possible to address in most cases given time and resources, as many of the 14–19 Pathfinders have shown. The latter, however, are more difficult to overcome and, as we have seen earlier in this chapter, are reinforced by powerful national policy levers.

TOWARDS A MORE STRONGLY COLLABORATIVE 14–19 APPROACH

Given these conditions, perhaps it is not surprising that across England as a whole, a recent Nuffield Report on 14–19 Education and Training

- Shared aims and values with clear remits for the organizations involved (e.g. Ofsted 2003b; Rodger, Cowen and Brass 2003; Higham and Yeomans 2005; Atkinson et al. 2007).
- A history and culture of collaboration locally (Aiston, Rudd and O'Donnell 2002; O'Donnell et al. 2006) including the role of strong local identities (Higham and Yeomans 2005).
- Strong and effective leadership and co-ordination (e.g. Nelson et al. 2001; Atkinson et al. 2007) and well trained and committed teaching staff (e.g. Ofsted 2004; Higham and Yeomans 2005; Atkinson et al. 2007).
- Good personal relationships between staff in different organizations (Munday and Fawcett 2002) with strong commitment to partnership working (Atkinson et al. 2007).
- Effective communication structures (Atkinson et al. 2007), particularly in relation to information on learner progress (e.g. Nelson et al. 2001; Golden et al. 2004).
- Equality between partners (Higham et al. 2004; Atkinson et al. 2007).
- Effective quality assurance systems and procedures for measuring a partnership's achievements (e.g. Audit Commission 1998; Ofsted 2004).
- Common timetabling (e.g. Ofsted/FEFC 1999; Higham et al. 2004).
- Access to additional funding to support collaboration (e.g. Nelson et al. 2001; Golden et al. 2004; Higham et al. 2004).

Figure 6.1 *Key factors supporting effective partnership working*

- The predominant influence of competition and selection as drivers of institutional provision and attitudes, exacerbated by cultural differences, misunderstandings and prejudices between institutions or sectors (e.g. Smith, Kerr and Harris 2003; ISC 2003; Adnett and Davies 2003; Higham et al. 2004; Higham and Yeomans 2005).
- Institutional distinctiveness and the fear of diluting institutional ethos (Aiston, Rudd and O'Donnell 2002; Higham et al. 2004).
- The lack of local leadership or co-ordination capacity, either at individual institutional or LEA/LLSC level (Higham and Yeoman 2005).
- Fragility because of a reliance on committed individuals (particularly heads and principals) whose work might disappear if they move to another area (Hayward et al. 2006).
- Procedural barriers to sharing information, such as the Data Protection Act, which make monitoring progress over time and across institutions very difficult (e.g. Ofsted 2004).
- Logistical complexities of partnership working (e.g. common timetabling, student transport and organizing staff meetings, particularly in rural locations) (Golden et al. 2004; Higham et al. 2004; Higham and Yeomans 2005).
- Lack of time and resources required for collaboration (e.g. Golden et al. 2004; Aiston, Rudd and O'Donnell 2002; Ofsted/FEFC 1999; Higham and Yeoman 2005).

Figure 6.2 *Factors inhibiting collaboration*

(Hayward et al. 2006) concluded that most partnerships were best described as 'weakly collaborative' when judged against six dimensions of partnership (see Table 6.1). These dimensions, which we have developed from research and observations of practice undertaken for the Nuffield Review, are briefly explained below and their relation to the wider 14–19 reform process is elaborated in Chapter 7.

For each of the dimensions in Table 6.1, in the first column we provide some examples of 14–19 developments that are taking place in different areas of the country due to the reform process. In columns two and three, we contrast more weakly and more strongly collaborative approaches to these practices. It is important to note that these approaches are not in opposition to one another but should be treated as a continuum, with 14–19 partnerships lying at different points on each of the six dimensions. Moreover, certain dimensions are more nationally constrained than others. In particular, the curriculum/qualifications and accountability dimensions are strongly determined by national policy and also shape the other four dimensions to a greater or lesser degree. Nevertheless, within these national constraints, 14–19 partnerships can take a more reactive or a more proactive stance depending on their confidence as a partnership and their educational philosophical position.

Dimension 1: Vision, purposes and underpinning principles

As discussed earlier, many of the studies on partnership working point to the importance of a shared educational vision with strong underpinning values and clearly articulated purposes for the 14–19 phase. These principles, which are often the starting points for local collaborative arrangements, provide the 'glue' that binds the wider actors together in preparing young people for adult life, further learning and work. The creation of a shared vision is not, however, about constructing an artificial or bureaucratic consensus. It recognizes that collaborative learning systems will bring together partners with different professional traditions and will, therefore, involve negotiation, debate and 'co-configuration' in which mutual learning takes place (Warmington et al. 2004). The wider literature on partnership and collaboration (for example Newman 2001; Frye and Webb 2002) points to the difficulties of this type of working, a situation compounded by the organizational complexity of the learning and skills sector as a whole (Hodgson et al. 2005b and 2007). Shared vision not only has to assist with the 'difficult' processes of partnership, but also has to create the will for more radical change.

Table 6.1 *Dimensions of weakly and strongly collaborative 14–19 learning systems*

Dimensions	Weakly collaborative	Strongly collaborative
1. Vision, purposes and underpinning principles For example • Vision statements for the curriculum and for 14–19 partnership • Learner entitlement statements	Vision statements and learner entitlements largely confined to the government agenda of providing 'alternative' learning experiences.	Vision statements and learner entitlements cover all aspects of 14–19 learning, including GCSEs and A Levels, and attempt to take a more unified and integrated approach to learning.
2. Curriculum, qualifications and assessment For example Mapping provision • Building progression routes • Deciding on a diploma offer • Strengthening vocational provision • Providing independent inform-ation, advice and guidance (IAG)	Development of vocational path-ways and programmes from 14+ for some learners. A primary goal is motivating disaffected 14–16-year-olds, using college and work-based provision. IAG compromised by institutional competition and used as a means of compensating for a transparent system.	Developing holistic programmes across all types of learning with a focus on more flexible, applied and practical approaches for all learners from 14+. IAG as both a strong entitlement for learners and as an integral part of a more planned and collaborative system.
3. Planning, funding, organization and governance in 'a local area' For example • Local Authorities (LAs), the Learning and Skills Council (LSC) and Connexions working together to deliver the entitlement • Forming partnerships and clusters • Developing local prospectuses • Making decisions about funding collaborative learning opportunities	Confused or contested relationships between LAs, the LSC and providers, with lack of clarity about local leadership. Partnerships and clusters are under-developed, dependent on external funding and easily destabilised (e.g. by institutional competition or changes in key personnel).	Clear and accepted local governance arrangements with a high degree of collaboration between LAs, LSC, local providers and wider partners (e.g. employers, voluntary and community organizations) thus increasing governance capacity and leadership.
4. Professionalism, pedagogy and leadership For example • 14–19 Pathfinders • Learning Visits • Development networks and joint continuing professional development (CPD)	Conformity to government reform agenda without a strong professionally informed sense of what is required at the local level. Limited leadership and CPD, with a dependence on nationally generated support and key local individuals.	Strong sense of local professionalism, leadership and a shared knowledge of the area; a more reflective, longer-term, planned and locally generated approach to capacity building using pooled local and national funding and locally agreed tariffs for learner programmes.
5. Physical learning environments and communications systems For example • Building new skills centres • Building Schools for the Future • Information and Communications Technology (ICT) infrastructure • Pooling funding for shared resources or specialisms	New infrastructure arrangements are driven by institutional self-interest and incentivised by national funding (e.g. vocational and ICT facilities developed on a competitive basis and dispersed across schools, colleges and work-based learning providers).	The development of institutional infrastructure, physical learning environments and communications to meet the needs of all learners in the local area. Institutional self-interest subordinate to area-wide agreements.
6. New accountability framework For example • Performance measures • Progression targets • Local quality assurance and improvement systems	National government steering mechanisms and policy (e.g. performance tables, targets and funding) continue to drive institutional self-interest and inhibit collaboration. Little development of local accountability mechanisms.	New government mechanisms (e.g. 14–19 entitlement, prospectus and progression targets) used to strengthen local accountability frameworks. Development of agreed local quality assurance systems and area-wide performance measures.

Dimension 2: Curriculum, qualifications and assessment

At the heart of strongly collaborative local learning systems lie curriculum, qualifications and assessment. It is possible to argue that those based on a unified curriculum and credit-based qualifications framework are more likely to be inclusive and effective because of the emphasis on what is common to learning for this phase as well as what choices learners can make. From a learner perspective, a learning system is one that creates clear demands but, at the same time, provides space to participate in the learning process from a position of interest and confidence. This requires impartial information advice and guidance (IAG), which is currently often compromised by institutional self-interest in a competitive environment. It has been recognized that the provision of independent IAG is under-developed (NAO 2007). Strongly collaborative systems would see IAG as an integral part of a more collectively planned approach to provision where it would be used to help young people to navigate the expanded offer available to them.

This unified approach to curriculum, qualifications and assessment will mean balancing features of coherence and national frameworks with choice, local determination and personalization. It also suggests the need for a new type of participative pedagogy and strong support for expansive learning in a variety of challenging contexts, including the workplace (Fuller and Unwin 2003). This is most likely to be facilitated by shifts in approaches to assessment away from the dominance of external examinations and towards the development of more teacher-directed assessment. Standards would be secured through local quality assurance systems involving a range of stakeholders, as well as by national awarding bodies and inspectors (Working Group on 14–19 Reform 2004a).

Dimension 3: Planning, funding, organization and governance in 'a local area'

The concept of a local learning area, capable of offering the full range of provision for all 14–19-year-olds, suggests the need for a high degree of agreement about what provision is offered and how funding will be used to support learners. Decisions will also have to be made about which partner has prime responsibility for different types of learning and how that learning will be recognized, particularly by employers in the local labour market and by higher education providers. Area planning would have to take precedence over individual institutional plans in the building of a more area-based approach.

As indicated earlier, however, the notion of a local learning area, in contrast to a local administrative area, is not well-established within the English education and training system. This is partly due to the impact of marketization and performance measures which have privileged the national and the individual institutional levels rather than local governance. It is thus the institution, not the area, that remains the object of delivery and accountability. In the development of strongly collaborative local learning systems, however, the focus would have to change to one where the performance of an area became dominant. This, as we discuss later in the chapter, raises significant questions about the level and type of governance arrangements required.

Dimension 4: Professionalism, pedagogy and leadership

The concept of a collaborative learning system with a strong area-based dimension requires a common set of education professional characteristics. These include a sharing of educational values around curriculum, pedagogy and leadership; a shared analysis of the needs of the learning area; joint professional development supported by greater equity of pay and conditions to encourage genuine collaborative delivery; and agreed approaches to specialized provision. Given the breadth of learning opportunities and support required for 14–19-year-olds, it is also important to consider the role of an 'expanded professionalism'. Education specialists, public sector professionals from other walks of life (for example social services, voluntary and community agencies and health) and those delivering work-based learning would seek opportunities to work together and learn from one another. However, as one of our interviewees pointed out, this would require strong forms of leadership and compromises in institutional autonomy:

> For collaboration to work, it has to be managed and, therefore, has to be led by somebody who has authority over the component parts so they can act in the interests of the learner ... this would mean giving up sovereignty by the providers. (PA 3)

Dimension 5: Physical learning environments and communications systems

The development of high-quality physical learning environments and the sharing of expensive specialist resources will play a crucial role in an effective local learning system. It makes sense to concentrate these resources in large tertiary institutions that actively involve employers. It does not seem to be economically viable or educationally sound to develop strongly vocational provision in individual schools because they do not have the vocational expertise and precious resources become dispersed. In strongly collaborative 14–19 local learning systems, schools would primarily provide general and pre-vocational education, although they might collaborate, as is already being planned in some areas (for example Ashford in Kent and the West Notts Learning Centre of Vocational Excellence), in the development and use of shared 'skills centres'.

High-quality 14–19 education and training will also require extensive collaboration around communications systems to track and support learner participation, achievement and progression. There are already examples of significant developments in ICT communications systems in which schools and colleges promote continuity between key stages, develop and share learning materials and provision and foster new ways of interacting with learners across the whole curriculum (for example Kingswood Partnership and Northumberland Virtual College). These are key to communication between consortia or tertiary providers, their feeder schools and wider partners, particularly in rural areas.

Dimension 6: A new accountability framework

As we have seen earlier, the accountability framework drives institutions in different directions, with some mechanisms promoting collaboration and others competition. Movement towards more strongly collaborative arrangements could involve tipping the balance of institutional incentives to ensure that potential partners are able to focus attention not only on their own institution and learners, but also on the 'learning area' and the attainment and development of all 14–19 learners within it, a point supported by the National Audit Office (2007). Potential measures might include:

- area-wide performance indicators for participation, achievement and progression that are monitored by Ofsted;
- shared quality assurance and improvement systems between partners;
- local area targets, developed on a 'bottom-up' basis by partnerships;
- funding incentives for collaborative provision and practices and greater clarity about funding learning which takes place across more than one site;
- local area inspections and reviews against specified criteria on collaboration;
- increased teacher involvement in local assessment of provision, based on

national processes of validation and institutional licensing;
- changes to 'rules of governance and accountability' (for example for governing bodies) that actively promote collaboration and reduce competition.

Several of our interviewees commented on the need for this shift, with one remarking:

> *I think if the Government can stiffen its sinews and bolster partnership working between schools and colleges with suitable funding incentives and suitable accountability measures, shared accountability measures, then we shall see everybody coming into the tent. (PA 19)*

Although there is now much greater encouragement through national policy initiatives for local 14–19 collaboration, the arrangements remain essentially voluntary and tied to government funding streams. Evidence suggests that their success depends very much on the enthusiasm and commitment of the partners and the calibre of the co-ordinators. Policy stresses the responsibility of localities to deliver the national 14–19 entitlement. However, effective practice cannot be achieved simply by a strong practitioner response to national policy, because there are aspects of it that continue to inhibit innovative local development. Therefore, the realization of 'strongly collaborative 14–19 local learning systems' will require the synergy of local innovation and national reform – the latter particularly in relation to qualifications, accountability and funding. For these reasons, it is important to see the institutional dimension of 14–19 education and training in England as part of the wider debates on governance and public service reform.

LEADERSHIP AND GOVERNANCE IN THE 14–19 PHASE

The move from weakly to strongly collaborative systems raises three important inter-related questions regarding leadership and governance of 14–19 education and training:

- What kind of system leadership is required so that all schools, colleges and work-based providers work together for the benefit of learners?
- What is the significance of LAs being given full strategic and funding responsibility for the 14–19 phase?
- What are the implications of wider developments in the relationship between national, regional and local governance?

Presently, collaboration between institutions is broadly a voluntary arrangement. Several recent accounts of collaborative activity in the 14–19 phase paint a cautious, if not pessimistic, picture as to how far arrangements can progress in the current governance environment. For example, Lumby and Morrison (2006) argue that, despite some evidence of altruism, institutional self-interest still dominates, leading to various forms of 'gaming' as 'partners' both compete and collaborate to gain advantage. Briggs et al. (2007), using evidence from four area case-studies, argue that 'collaborative leadership' is being constrained by power agendas and cultural differences between institutions. They also suggest that the emphasis on system or collaborative leadership is underdeveloped, compared to that of leadership of single organizations.

Both sets of authors conclude that supra-organizational goals will have to be reinforced if the balance of relationships is to be tipped in favour of collaboration. Briggs and colleagues go on to argue that factors that work for partnership (for example alignment of organizational goals and a sense of common purpose) will have to be strengthened by government resources targeted at collaboration and that there has to be stability of the wider governance environment. The implications we draw from these studies are that simply fostering collaborative leadership within partnerships, while important, will be insufficient to increase joint work to the point that local 'areas' can effectively meet the needs of all 14–19 learners. Something has to happen from without.

Suddenly LAs are back in favour after years of neglect and hostility from successive administrations. From 2010, they become responsible for funding as well as oversight of 14–19 education. This can be regarded as a long overdue move to provide more democratic legitimacy for post-compulsory education, which has been lacking since the late-1980s. Giving LAs strategic powers in relation to 14–19 may be a move in the right direction of democratic accountability, but may not empower them to reshape institutional relations. How far will they be able to deliver the kind of collaborative leadership and governance environment suggested by the needs of strongly collaborative local learning systems? While it is obviously too early to tell, there are a number of issues looming. The first is whether LAs will have the capacity for leadership. Presently, many, particularly 'unitaries', are small and lack sufficient specialist staff to lead 14–19 developments. It would make sense for local LSC partnership teams to become part of LAs after 2010 to bring in expertise on funding and post-16 learning.

But more importantly, it is not clear whether LAs will have the backing of key policy levers. By themselves, LAs may not have the power nor the credibility to provide leadership on the scale needed to bring all local partners into a more deliberative planning process to meet the Government's own targets for participation. The twin problems of expertise and power were summed by one of our interviewees:

> I mean there is an expertise problem at the moment because their capacity has been whittled away. But if that were overcome, you'd still have the question, what authority have they got? If they actually believed if a member of a collaborative partnership was not pulling its weight, or was simply not good enough, what's their authority? (PA 3)

Outside of 14–19 education, the debate about devolution of greater powers to local government has been raging for several years, with far-reaching implications for creating more collaborative local learning environments (Spours et al. 2007b). At the same time, the regional agenda is steadily taking shape. In London, Mayor Ken Livingstone has created a London-wide Skills and Employment Board to support learning for adults. A strong case is emerging for aspects of 14–19 education also to be co-ordinated on a London Region basis to facilitate greater learner access to specialist vocational facilities, to recognize complex travel-to-learn patterns across the capital and to prepare young people for jobs available in a metropolitan labour market (Grainger et al. 2007). The Mayor's Office is consulting on this (LSEB 2007). Elsewhere, the Government's vision for regional governance will see more integration and alignment of agencies at the regional level; a process which appears to be preparing regions for a greater role in the future (NLGN 2007). It would appear, therefore, that devolution of responsibilities between national, regional and local government is on the move, but the patterns are not yet clear and important political barriers remain.

CONCLUSION

While 14–19 collaborative arrangements at the local level have made significant progress in the recent period, the evidence we have drawn on suggests that it will be difficult to see much further movement in the current governance and resourcing environment. There are simply too many systemic factors stacked against collaborative activity. Despite the difficulties, we think there is a very strong case for a step change in institutional collaboration to serve the needs of all 14–19-year-olds if they are to be fully supported to participate successfully in education and training up to the age of 18.

However, the way in which collaboration is seen will have to change. Currently, the prevailing view is that it is about some providers working together to support some learners. Given government aims for participation, it should be all providers working together to support all learners, not just to improve participation rates but also to ensure the quality of what is achieved.

We conclude, therefore, with an argument for three inter-related changes. First, the scope of collaboration needs to be broadened to include learners in general, not just vocational education. Those studying GCSEs and A Levels also need access to wider learning environments and new educational challenges if they are to develop the breadth of skills and knowledge for the future. In this sense, there is a clear link between qualifications and organizational reform. Second, and this point has been made repeatedly throughout the chapter, incentives and accountability systems for collaboration have to become more powerful than those for competition. This we link not just to the role of LAs, but also to the development of a more devolved system of governance with greater powers at both local and regional levels to bring social partners together in collaborative action. Finally, and most controversially, partnership and collaboration has to be about creating more coherent, equitable and effective local systems, not about avoiding important decisions regarding post-16 reorganization. Delivering efficiency gains and greater social equity is about strongly collaborative local learning systems based on both greater diversity of provision and on stronger, larger and more versatile institutions.

NOTES

[1] By the term 'organization' we are referring to the providers of 14–19 education and their relationships with one another. The term 'governance' refers to the wider political and administrative relationships between national, regional, local and institutional levels.

[2] The Government's aim, under *Every Child Matters*, 'is for every child, whatever their background or their circumstances, to have the support they need to be healthy, stay safe, enjoy and achieve, make a positive contribution, achieve economic well-being': www.everychildmatters.gov.uk/aims/ accessed 9 November 2007.

[3] On 5 November 2007, the Secretary of State announced that the September Guarantee would be extended to 17-year-olds (DCFS News Release 2007/0198, *Raising the participation age – four building blocks.*

chapter 7

THE FUTURE OF THE 14–19 PHASE IN ENGLAND

The prognosis for a coherent and enduring 14–19 phase of education and training in England lies in the balance. On the one hand, there are strong arguments for its existence. These coalesce around the case for an uninterrupted upper secondary education from the age of 14 to the age of 18/19 to help young people make a successful transition from school to adult and working life. The idea of an extended phase was formalized by the Government's announcement that it intended to the raise the participation age to 18 by 2015. On the other hand, this laudable aim is confronted by a formidable set of practical, structural and cultural barriers. Moreover, as we have seen, there is no settled view about the way forward in either the short or longer term.

For these reasons, we begin the chapter where we began the book, with a review of the case for a strong and viable 14–19 phase. This is followed by a summary of the defining features of 14–19 education and training in England, including the Government's approach to policy and innovation. We argue that the current strategy will not create a strong and enduring 14–19 phase. In the final part of the chapter we look to the future by outlining proposals that can overcome tensions and contradictions in government policy and harness local innovation in order to address deepseated problems in the English system.

THE IMPORTANCE OF 14–19

The 23 policy actors we interviewed for this book (see Chapter 1) all agreed about the need for a 14–19 phase. It was treated as a 'given'. While this may partly be because it is seen as a government priority, there was undoubted support for the 'idea' of a phase that spanned compulsory and (what is still) post-compulsory education in an attempt to overcome the effects of the current 16+ divide. What our interviewees wanted to talk about was the 'approach' to the phase and how it should be organized.

As we have suggested in Chapter 1, and as these interviews confirm, the major aim of this new phase is to raise levels of participation and attainment. The Government emphasizes the skills case. It argues that to remain globally competitive, more young people and adults will need to acquire the necessary skills and qualifications to gain employment and to become economically useful. This 'participation and attainment case' was broadly accepted by all our interviewees, reflecting a bottom-line consensus for the creation of a 14–19 phase.

Similarly, there is support for a social cohesion and social justice argument for a 14–19 phase which links education, skill formation, employment and poverty reduction. There is clear evidence that those young people who stay longer in education and gain any level of qualification are more likely to be in employment than those who do not (Macintosh 2004). Moreover, the higher the qualification, the greater the economic returns for learning. In addition, there are wider individual and social benefits of learning in terms of outcomes such as health, civic participation and crime reduction (Schuller et al. 2004). Those who carry on longer in formal education and training are also more likely to participate in lifelong learning (Sargant and Aldridge 2002). Interviewees saw the intimate connection between 14–19 and future learning. As one put it: 'its sole mission should be to encourage learning for life and it isn't just a question of "thank God I can finish learning at that age"' (PA 9).

There is a third argument for an extended upper secondary phase, which focuses on young people and how they experience education. This has prompted the Nuffield 14–19 Review to ask questions about the fundamental aims and purposes of the phase (Hayward et al. 2006). From this perspective, there is something distinctive about learners between the ages of 14–19 because they are seeking to develop their own identity at a period of transition between childhood and adulthood. At this point, as one of our interviewees commented, 'they start thinking about their futures and thinking about entering into adult life' (PA 14). This argument suggests the need for an approach to pedagogy that stresses experiences beyond the classroom to expand learner horizons, to help them engage with wider society and to provide them with the tools to make effective choices during this important period of transition.

Many of our interviewees articulated what might be seen as a fourth major argument for a reformed 14–19 phase because of their desire to address long-standing structural, educational and cultural barriers to effective and equitable participation and attainment. They voiced concerns about selection and division in the English education system, which begins to present itself at the age of 11 with secondary transfer, can become more evident at Key Stage 4, but crystallises at 16 around the transition between compulsory and post-compulsory education. As we have noted in earlier chapters, this is the point at which young people are channelled into either academic or vocational learning and into a school sixth form, college or work-based learning environment. In the current system, this is not a 'neutral' set of decisions. One route, the general/academic, is of higher status and is recognized to make the most positive difference to your life chances. The argument for a 14–19 phase thus becomes one about the academic/vocational divide, the effects of choice and the 16+ transition in sustaining or combating social division. This is why 14–19 education and training is such a socially and politically combustible arena.

For these reasons, the aims and purposes of a 14–19 phase are contested in the English context. Most people could sign up to the first three purposes, although they might rank them differently, but it is the fourth that is the centre of controversy. It was this area that interviewees wanted to talk about because their arguments for a 14–19 phase focused on how it should be organized. For many, the raison d'être for the phase is to change the existing educational order from one dominated by selection and division to one focused on progression and equity. For others, it is a case of trying to create more effective choices in a divided system. Later in the chapter, we will briefly explore these different perspectives, but we will argue that only a more unified and comprehensive upper secondary system will deliver the necessary change. But before doing so, we want to draw together the themes from the previous chapters and the interviews to characterize 14–19 arrangements and the strengths and weaknesses of the Government's current policy approach.

THE 14–19 SYSTEM IN ENGLAND

In earlier chapters we have argued that there has been a distinctive English approach to upper secondary education over the last 20 years and that the current government reforms broadly conform to this tradition (see Figure 7.1).

- Education-based and largely rooted in schools (hence the powerful cultural symbol of sixth forms), even though many young people study in FE colleges and with work-based training providers (see Chapter 2).
- Qualifications-led because of the role of accreditation in defining the learning experience of young people and in measuring the outcomes of the phase (see Chapter 2).
- Track-based – three main types of qualifications (A Levels/GCSEs, broad vocational qualifications, including the first 14 lines of new Diplomas, and NVQ-based apprenticeship programmes) define the three main tracks – general, broad vocational and work-based/occupational (see Chapters 3–5).
- Dominated by a selective general education based on individual qualifications (GCSEs and A Levels) with no common 'leaving' or 'graduation' certification at the age of 18/19 (see Chapter 3).
- Having a 'reactive' vocational education that is largely determined by the selective academic track and weak employer engagement, compelling it to take on social inclusion functions (see Chapters 4 and 5).
- Containing a small work-based track caught in a low-supply, low-status, low-visibility and low-quality syndrome (see Chapter 5).
- Complex and competitive in terms of institutional arrangements and in which 14–19 partnerships remain 'weakly collaborative' (see Chapter 6).
- Retaining a strong break at 16+ in terms of curriculum and qualifications, institutional arrangements and governance (see Chapters 1 and 6);
- Dominated by a strong national-institutional governance dynamic with a weaker role for local and regional governance (see Chapters 1 and 6).
- Shaped by powerful external forces such as higher education and employers which exert a largely conservative influence (see Chapter 1).
- Market-based and socially competitive, making it highly politicized (see Chapters 1 and 2).
- Constantly being reformed with little real change to its basic features (see Chapter 2).

Figure 7.1 *Key characteristics of the English approach to the 14-19 phase*

The sum total of these key features leads us to conclude that the 14–19 phase in England is still fragile and largely remains a policy aspiration. The phase has little to hold it together, being dominated by distinctions between academic and vocational learning; by a 16+ curricular and organizational divide; by institutional autonomy and competition; and by the lack of constructive or sustained engagement of key partners such as higher education and employers. There are, of course, counter-trends coming from national policy, for example, the raising of the participation age and the September Guarantee; functional skills as a form of common learning; the statutory 14–19 Entitlement; and the demands of the Diplomas for partnership working. However, these constitute a relatively weak and subordinate set of forces when pitted against the deep-seated historical features of the system. The complexity of the 14–19 phase and its low public recognition arise from the combination of these dominant and subordinate features and policies, as the Government seeks to implement reforms while leaving the basic divisive structures of the system relatively undisturbed. In the eyes of an interviewee, this leads to the perverse English system strength of second chance:

> Until we move on from the elite thing, we'll be bedevilled, you know. We'll privilege some at the expense of others and then we'll kind of wring our hands and worry, and a lot of our work will be concerned with helping the people who've been screwed over by the system to pick themselves up, brush themselves down and have choices later on. (PA 15)

THE GOVERNMENT'S APPROACH TO 14–19 REFORM

Hall's (2003) seminal work on 'New Labour's double-shuffle' helps us to understand the complexity of policy, how policy tensions arise and what Lumby and Foskett (2007) describe as 'turbulence without change'. He characterizes New Labour's approach to policy and policy-making as a 'hybrid regime' of dominant neo-liberal and subordinate social democratic strands of discourse. The dominant strands involve the continued use of new public management, for example, the restructuring of the public sector through privatization and competition and drives to improve efficiency by means of performance measurement and auditing. The subordinate strands contain more social democratic aims, such as promoting increased expenditure on education, concern about those young people not in employment, education or training (NEETs). These two agendas, operating together, have produced what Newman (2001) refers to as an 'adaptive form of neo-liberalism', capable of change, while preserving the existing order. The concept of the 'double shuffle' can help to explain the Government's policy in the three main areas we have focused on in this book: curriculum and qualifications, organization and governance, and employers and the labour market.

The Government argues that it wants to improve 14–19 education and training by introducing a wider range of provision to benefit more learners and to raise levels of participation. Since 2002, there has been a gradual diversification of Key Stage 4 through the introduction of a range of vocational and applied qualifications and learning opportunities. From 2005, however, the major thrust of government policy has been directed towards the design and implementation of the 14 (and now 17) Diploma lines. As we explained in Chapter 4, the Diplomas are not only intended to provide choice of provision, but also a new form of pedagogy and programmes of learning. At the same time, however, the Government has accepted that A Levels and GCSEs should remain the 'cornerstones' of the 14–19 curriculum (see Chapter 3). This effectively means that the Diplomas will be seen as an 'alternative' to the general educational mainstream. In the area of qualifications, the double shuffle helps us to understand why the Government did not adopt the Tomlinson proposals, in which all qualifications for 14–19-year-olds would have become part of a single unified diploma system, but chose instead to introduce something new into the existing divided system. This particular combination of policy leads us to characterize the Government's approach to curriculum and qualifications as 'pragmatic track-based'.

The same type of analysis can be applied to organization and governance. Competition between institutions dominates 14–19 education and training, with collaboration between of providers a weaker strand of policy (see Chapter 6). Moreover, the institutional motives for collaboration are both progressive and regressive. On the one hand, collaboration can provide greater choice of provision and bring a more shared sense of working together for a common cause. On the other, in its current form, collaboration can simply preserve the existing order by catering for a minority outside the GCSE and A Level regime and by providing small and inefficient school sixth forms with a lifeline. Partnership working is thus both innovative and an excuse for not taking stronger action to rationalize provision.

In the area of governance, there are still tensions between the dominant pattern – national steering of institutional behaviour – and the newer but subordinate move towards a stronger role for local authorities as part of the democratic devolution agenda. For 14–19 education and training this creates a tension between institutional autonomy and a focus on learners in an individual provider and a weaker more planned approach to the organization of learning for all young people in a locality. When this is combined with local authorities' limited resources, capacity and power to manage 14–19, the result is insufficient local leadership to bring about effective organizational change.

With regard to the labour market, the Government's strategy relies on voluntarism to promote employer involvement (see Chapter 5). It has given employers a front seat in the design of the Diplomas and continually exhorts them to get involved in education and training, most recently through the Employers' Pledge. But this voluntarist approach does not lead to sustained engagement. Moreover, it relies on learners asserting their rights. So, while young employees are included as part of the strategy for raising the participation age, it is only those young people employed for more than 20 hours who are entitled to time off for training and they will need to have the confidence to persuade their employers to release them. The Government's reliance on voluntarism, which places demands on learners but appeals to employers' social conscience, simply delays the day when more regulation of the youth labour market will be deemed necessary.

Overall, the Government's adaptive approach to 14–19 reform, in which it pursues both dominant and subordinate agendas, results in complexity, confusions and policy tensions, making it difficult for those involved in the implementation process. Practitioners, local authority employees, Learning and Skills Council (LSC) officials and other national policy-makers all want the reforms to succeed for the sake of learners, even if they have different degrees of reservation about how far piecemeal and even contradictory policies will work. The adaptive strategy is a world of half-measures, which can be viewed as either half-full or half-empty. Those who adopt a half-full perspective, focusing on the subordinate social-democratic strands of policy, would see government as taking a modest step in the right direction. They hope that a particular initiative, such as the Diplomas, might have a significant impact on participation and attainment in the 14–19 system. The half-empty perspective, on the other hand, would place reform proposals in their wider historical and system context, leading to a more pessimistic assessment of the power of a single measure to effect system change. The issue is whether what we have termed 'half measures' can become the steps and stages of an explicit and comprehensive long-term vision and strategy. This approach would require recognizing the undoubted strengths of the English system – bottom-up innovation, flexibility and the possibility of a second chance – in order to build on areas of success and to maximize consensus for enduring change while, at the same time, addressing fundamental historical and system weaknesses.

The English education and training system, despite its drift towards centralism over the last two decades, has a long record of local innovation (see Chapter 2). In terms of its approach to 14–19 reform, the Government recognizes that localities will experience different challenges and will have to tailor their strategies accordingly. It is, therefore, up to local partnerships to decide how to deal with key delivery issues such as governance arrangements (for example the co-ordination roles between local authorities, LSCs, institutions and wider stakeholders), the common curriculum framework, transport and so on. Schools, colleges and work-based learning providers, sometimes under the leadership of Local Authorities and the LSC, have seen the various 14–19 initiatives that have emerged since 2002 as opportunities to meet the needs of learners who do not find GCSEs and A Levels motivational. This has resulted in new and positive experiences for an important minority of learners not well-served by the current system. As we have argued in Chapter 6, however, local innovation has its limitations and ultimately can only flourish when it finds itself in a reciprocal relationship with national policy and key national steering mechanisms. A rich synergy between the national and the local is required to harness practitioner innovation and practical expertise in the gradual move towards a sustainable national 14–19 phase. An interviewee, with an intimate knowledge of national/local relations, stated: 'I think that people have their weather eye on support at national level to make their job easier at local level ... it's all very well at the local level, but people are looking to national decisions for support' (PA 23).

THE FUTURE OF 14–19 IN ENGLAND

Perspectives on reform

The general mood amongst the 23 policy-makers we interviewed was of regret that a golden opportunity to make a real impact on 14–19 education and training had been lost in 2005 with the rejection of the Tomlinson Report. For this reason, most expressed scepticism about the Government's 14–19 reforms. While they saw the rationale for a 14–19 phase and were pleased that the Government had focused attention on this area, in different ways and to varying degrees, they were critical of the Government approach to policy. The majority singled out for criticism divisions within the system with many doubting whether the Diplomas would make a serious impact when the GCSE/A Level route remained intact. They also mentioned the difficulties of 14–19 partnership working and the tensions between competition and collaboration. In addition, several were deeply concerned about implementation issues, including the speed of the reforms and the lack of time for reflection. Having said this, there was a widespread feeling that the announcement of the three new Diploma lines in science, languages and humanities was a step in the right direction, in so far as it signalled the Government's concern about the academic/vocational divide.

Looking back over the interview transcripts, it was apparent that interviewees felt more able to criticise the Government's 14–19 reforms than to articulate a coherent way forward. People were aware that it was not possible simply to turn the clock back to 2004, much as many would have liked to have done so. One interviewee summed up the mood:

> I think when Tomlinson had a groundswell of people behind him, it felt unanimous and it felt unstoppable. And, in a sense, that was because there was passion in the way that Mike and the people who worked with him described the whole thing. They weren't just committed, they were passionately committed. And it wasn't just the right thing to do, it was the only thing to do. (PA 1)

What interviewees argued for were features of a future system, many of which had formed part of the Tomlinson proposals – personalization, the use of credit, a common core to both skills and personal development, the idea of a climbing frame to promote progression, inter-locking levels between diplomas, Entry Level Diplomas, less external assessment, a stronger apprenticeship route, a coherent vision for the future and a policy framework that clearly encouraged collaboration and allowed professionals a stronger voice in all aspects of the policy process. A minority also argued explicitly for a single diploma framework for all 14–19 qualifications.

What the majority of our interviewees were not so clear about, however, was how to move from the current position to the kind of future they wanted or how their particular concerns could become part of an overall strategy. In this, they were reflecting the paradoxes of an implementation phase in which practitioners and policy-makers are morally bound to use their expertise to promote change, even if they realize the limitations and contradictions of the reforms. In Chapter 4, we have referred to those who take this position as 'pragmatic unifiers', in so far as they want to move towards a more inclusive national system in the long term but have to make current reforms work in order to meet the needs of their students in the short term.

While researchers are not a breed apart, we do have the luxury to stand back and ask difficult questions. In our view, however, we also have the duty to be constructive and to suggest ways forward based on historical and system-wide perspectives (Hodgson and Spours 2006b). This approach has led us to see ourselves as 'systemic unifiers' in relation to 14–19 reform. We, therefore, devote the final part of this book to the articulation of a comprehensive national reform approach containing many, if not all, of the features mentioned in the interviews, together with suggested evolutionary steps towards its realization.

First, however, we revisit an historical observation. Despite the amount of reform that has taken place over the last decade or more, the policy choices to be faced in 2008 and beyond remain as clear as they were in the early 1990s. How can 14–19 education and training be turned from a competitive battleground (Lumby and Foskett 2005) into an area of common purpose; from a focus on recycling partial policies centred around vocational education (Higham and Yeomans 2007a) to system-wide reform of all forms of learning; and from a selective approach, which benefits some learners, to a comprehensive phase which promotes progression for all?

Moving forward will require a break with much of the neo-liberal policy-making of the last 20 years. At the same time, a new mode of reform will have to be evolutionary and build on the strengths of the system, reflecting what we have termed elsewhere 'strategic gradualism' (Hodgson and Spours 2003). By the term 'strategic' we mean sustainable reform, which is guided by a strong and clearly articulated vision, together with an explicit set of principles to which all social partners can contribute. Gradualism suggests the need for deliberation and the capacity to engage in policy learning. It is important to take time to get the main principles and system design right and then to use experimentation and reflection to ensure effective implementation. Furthermore, a slower process safeguards those who are on the sharp end of change, particularly learners and teachers.

A UNIFIED 14–19 SYSTEM: RATIONALE, PRINCIPLES AND DIMENSIONS

Throughout the book we have described the negative impact of a divided curriculum and qualifications approach to 14–19 education and training. We have argued for solutions that reduce division between academic and vocational learning, minimize competitiveness between providers and tackle the lack of engagement of social partners outside education, notably employers and higher education providers. In doing so, we have referred to the need for a more unified approach to the organization of the 14–19 phase. Until this point in the book, we have analyzed the system in terms of its major constituent parts, because these reflect our triple-track system and the government's reform approach. Here, however, it is important to see the system as a whole in order to ensure that the reform of one area has a positive and symbiotic relationship with reform in another. This is why we have argued for many years, and again in this book, for a unified vision comprising the simultaneous reform of general and vocational education, allied to organizational and labour market changes (see Figure 7.2). A system-wide approach towards reform might also help address criticisms from colleagues who suggest that 'unification' is a naïve strategy that has taken insufficient notice of wider societal and sociological factors (for example Young 2008).

Vision: to create a unified, comprehensive, equitable and high-quality upper secondary phase of education for all 14–19-year-olds, involving a wide range of social partners, to meet the needs of 21st century society.

1. *A unified and inclusive system* – a single multi-level system of certification from Entry Level, which embraces general and vocational achievement for 14–19-year-olds in all learning contexts.
2. *Entitlement and cohesion* – a common core of learning for all 14–19-year-olds to develop knowledge, skills and attributes for successful learning, progression and active citizenship.
3. *Breadth, choice and specialization* – a qualifications and organizational framework to support breadth, depth and 'effective' curriculum choice underpinned by independent information, advice and guidance.
4. *A focus on progression* – a flexible, non-age-related, credit-based qualifications 'climbing frame' to promote both horizontal and vertical progression across the phase and to articulate with lifelong learning.
5. *The mutual improvement of general and vocational education* – the linked reform of general education (making it more inclusive, practical and challenging) and vocational education (associating it more closely with employment and raising its status with learners and employers).
6. *Assessment for learning* – focusing assessment on empowering learners and improving learning outcomes, rather than on emphasizing selection and accountability.
7. *Strong local learning systems* – creating strongly collaborative organizational arrangements from 14+ reinforced by supportive governance and accountability frameworks.
8. *Equity and efficiency* – approaches to resourcing that recognize the greater needs of the most disadvantaged; provide equity of conditions for those working across the 14–19 phase and promote efficient allocation through rationalized post-16 organization.
9. *A 'learning' policy process* – a deliberative and reflective approach to policy-making, capable of learning from professional experience, from the past and from international comparison.
10. *System-wide change* – a new curriculum and qualifications framework, supported by reciprocal institutional, governance and labour market reforms.

Figure 7.2 *A unified vision and 10 key principles for a 14–19 phase*

If division is our major historical problem then, arguably, unification must be our future solution. By unification we do not mean uniformity. A unified system along the lines outlined Figure 7.2 offers the possibility of balancing common forms of learning, which all young people need for the future, with choices and opportunities for specialization that develop individuals' talents and interests. It is, therefore, clear that by balancing commonality and diversity, unification does not mean a 'one-size fits all' approach. Unification of this type provides a means of ensuring that all learners have common experiences that underpin social cohesion but are also encouraged to experiment and to pursue their passions through choice and specialization.

Reform based on this vision and the 10 principles will require holistic and inter-related changes on at least four fronts: curriculum and qualifications; institutional organization and governance; engagement of social partners and labour market arrangements; and the reform of the policy process. The question is how these can be co-ordinated and realistically addressed in steps and stages over time to create an effective and enduring 14–19 phase. In our view, the leading strand should be curriculum and qualifications because these provide the educational values and purposes that the other three dimensions need to support.

Curriculum, qualifications and learning

In a unified system, learners should experience a common core of knowledge and skills, as well as the opportunity to specialize. General education will need to change. We support the Nuffield Review's argument (Hayward et al. 2006) that general education, while retaining a strong disciplinary knowledge and skills base, should also become more applied, practical and experiential, thus connecting it better to the modern world. All learners, regardless of their level of ability, would benefit. Furthermore, as we have argued earlier, this shift in the nature of secondary schooling would allow vocational and work-based learning to assume its proper place as a preparation for and an engagement with the labour market, rather than becoming a refuge for young people disengaged from a narrow and selective general education. However, vocational learning, as international comparison suggests, would also need to contain a strong strand of general education to provide both greater levels of skill formation and enhanced progression opportunities to higher study (Green 1998). We, therefore, see a unification strategy leading to the simultaneous strengthening of both general and vocational education.

Given the dominant role that qualifications play in the English education system, we believe that the curriculum principles we have described above need to be embodied in a comprehensive qualifications framework that is able to promote breadth and depth of learning, together with clear and flexible progression opportunities. As we have argued elsewhere, these broad aims are best supported by a unified diploma system that combines features of baccalaureates and credit-based approaches (Hodgson et al. 2006). The former are notable for their ability to provide coherence and breadth of learning, while the latter are viewed as supporting flexibility, choice and the gradual accumulation of achievement.

In our interviews, strong support was voiced for a more flexible and life-long-oriented 14–19 phase with criticism of the Government's emphasis on a 19+ divide:

> It seems to me an anomaly to separate out what 14–19s are doing from adults. The way in which the qualifications framework should operate is precisely to blur these watersheds at every stage of learning development, so you don't get to the age of 16 and education stops because you've completed a section and you've got to commit yourself to starting all over again with a new level ... that's the way to lose people and achieve drop-out. What you want is the continuity. (PA 14)

This sentiment translated into support for a credit-based 'climbing frame' (PA 22), which provides 'regular, incremental awards, so that young people remain engaged and remain being rewarded for what they're doing' (PA 1). Interviewees also talked about 'transferability' (PA 12).

The Tomlinson proposals for a unified diploma system represented the most public rendition to date of the twin aims of coherence and flexibility, although since then the idea of blending of grouped awards and credit has been explored further, and the Qualifications and Credit Framework (QCF) presents a new landscape for reform (Hodgson et al. 2006). In Figure 7.3 we summarize the main messages from the Tomlinson reports, but in doing so we recognize that the reform process has moved on since 2004. Similarly, we do not feel bound by the Tomlinson proposals. In important respects, we seek to go beyond them in our outline of the key features of a possible future unified English Diploma system.

The power of these proposals radically to alter 14–19 education and training depends on introducing them as a holistic package. It is only when the proposals work symbiotically that the features of the unified multi-level diploma system can tackle the barriers in the present system – lack of motivation and disengagement, weak vocational qualifications, division, selection and academic elitism. One of our interviewees had a very specific image of a diploma that addressed division:

> So I've always thought, the way forward for England would be to have something that was called something recognizable like the 'Advanced Diploma' that you could get through a variety of routes and slowly but surely try and dissolve those routes from within. (PA 10)

- *Four levels* – Entry to Advanced and which interlock (e.g. an Intermediate Level English Diploma would require a majority of attainment at Level 2, but would also allow the accreditation of some Level 1 and Level 3 learning). This would encourage both breadth and progression.
- *Common Core* of knowledge and skills comprising at least English, Mathematics, ICT, a Modern Foreign Language, Citizenship and Community Action and Service, and, of course, an Extended Project, although the size of the Core and the proportions of each of its component parts could vary according to level and type of Diploma.
- *Two types of diplomas*, open/general and specialized/named, cutting across all forms of learning in the 14–19 phase. Specialized/named diplomas should only be available post-16 in order to prevent premature specialization and to allow for learner maturation. For example, 14–16-year-olds could attend college or a workplace for a proportion of their learning week, as part of their attainment of an open/general diploma, but they would not be confined to a particular sector or occupation. English Diplomas, in their specialized/named form, would also have the capacity to be used as a learning framework for apprenticeships.
- *Credit* as the currency of the English Diploma system. Learner achievement would be recorded as a combination of credits, grades and narrative, listed on a diploma transcript. This paper or/and electronic document would be cumulative, could be summarized at key transition points and used to promote progression.
- *Accreditation of the whole learner programme* in order to recognize the broad variety of learning activities and experiences within and beyond the classroom.
- *Utilization of existing qualifications and components*, thus building on the strengths of the current qualifications system and allowing for a gradual transition process.
- *Assessment for learning* to ensure recognition of learning in different contexts; provide a greater role for teacher professional judgment (although external examinations would remain at key points) and reduce the assessment burden of the current system. Professional assessment could be led by 'chartered assessors' working in collaboration with national awarding bodies, the inspectorate and accredited colleges/employers.
- *Information, advice and guidance* to be built into the diploma entitlement to support effective choice and progression within and beyond the diploma system.

Figure 7.3 *Design features of an English Diploma system*

Institutional organization and governance – developing local learning systems

As we argued in Chapter 6, an important part of the 14–19 unified vision is the coherence of local organizational arrangements. We suggested that it was important to focus on the relationship between what we have called 'strongly collaborative local learning systems', involving more devolved forms of governance and improving the capacity of partners to work together locally. We also identified six dimensions of such a system:

1. Vision, purposes and underpinning principles.
2. Curriculum, qualifications and assessment.
3. Planning, funding, organization and governance in a 'local area'.
4. Professionalism, pedagogy and leadership.
5. Physical learning environments and communications systems.
6. A new accountability framework.

Over the two years since the 2005 14–19 White Paper, significant progress has been made on dimensions 1, 3, 4 and 5, because these have been largely within the control of 14–19 partnerships, although even here achievements have been limited. In our view, successful future reform will need to be based on a more reciprocal relationship between innovative local solutions and powerful national levers. In this respect, and considering the differential progress being made along the six dimensions, we think that attention has to be focused on four areas in particular – curriculum and qualifications, organizational planning and rationalization, funding and accountability.

In terms of curriculum and qualifications and their organizational implications, our central argument has been to focus collaboration on developing learning opportunities for *all* 14–19-year-olds, not just those on vocational courses. This would mean local strategies to deliver greater choice and quality of provision for those at the lower levels, as well as ensuring that all Advanced Level learners gained wider educational experience in the community and working life. This more comprehensive approach to curriculum and pedagogy would provide the opportunity for a wider range of teachers, college lecturers and work-based trainers to collaborate locally around these improvements. An obvious starting point would be the 14–19 Extended Project, which would be an entitlement for all learners in the English Diploma System, and would provide a focus of collaboration for both continuing professional development and assessment.

A more inclusive and comprehensive approach to reform could deliver two changes which elude us presently. First, it would bring all teachers and institutions into the 14–19 reform process because it would involve a new approach to general education, as well as new strands of vocational learning. Second, and precisely because of this, a comprehensive approach would focus attention back onto what schools themselves might offer to engage a wider range of learners. While we recognize the importance that some 14–16-year-olds currently attach to learning in places other than schools, the sheer scale of learner movement envisaged under the Government's Diploma system is uneconomical, unsustainable and difficult to defend educationally. We reiterate our argument that general education should be organized to prevent disaffection and unnecessary reasons for learner travel. The *Building Schools for the Future* capital funding initiative appears to offer a new scale of opportunity for schools to create more innovative and engaging learning environments which, when combined with the unified curriculum and qualifications reform we highlighted earlier, would allow new and motivational approaches to pedagogy. We think a general principle should be that young people should only travel for educational experiences that cannot be found within these new learning environments. They should not be travelling simply because they are fed up with school.

There is a case for planning new environments on an area basis so that specialisms could become available locally and learners would need to travel for access to these. Presently many schools are collaborating around A Level provision because their own sixth forms are too small to offer the choice learners need, but as we have explained in Chapter 6, these arrangements are often not cost-effective and involve unnecessary travel. There does not appear to be any strong evidence as yet that post-16 collaborative arrangements of this type improve examination results. Allied to this, and as part of strongly collaborative local learning systems, we think it is important to consider the extension of post-16 tertiary arrangements, which can combine economies of scale with high performance and social inclusion.

Any new system has to be underpinned by an effective and equitable funding mechanism. In this respect, strongly collaborative local learning systems would require a number of shifts. First, there would need to be more funding invested in learners who are in the lower levels of the system, because they require more support to progress, and in vocational learning, because it is more expensive than general education. Second, it would be important to ensure equity of pay and conditions between lecturers, teachers and work-based providers working with 14–19-year-olds. There is a moral and educational case that those with the same level of professional qualifications should be treated equally. Third, there would need to be a common, simplified and stable funding mechanism which incentivized collaborative working rather than competition.

Local learning systems will need area-wide accountability measures to provide common goals for partnership institutions and to combat competitive behaviour. These could include area-wide performance indicators for participation, achievement and progression, monitored by Ofsted; shared quality assurance and improvement systems between partners; local area targets, developed on a 'bottom-up' basis by partnerships; and local area inspections and reviews against specified criteria on partnership working.

Creating local learning systems will mean developing new balances of governance between five levels: national, regional, local, consortia and institutional. We think there is a case for the principle of 'subsidiarity': that decisions should be made as close to the learner as possible unless there is a good reason to do otherwise. The reality, however, is that different decisions will need to be made at each of the five levels. National government should set the broad narratives and frameworks for policy and, in doing so, enable regional and local government to play a stronger role in 14–19 education and training. The regional level, particularly in metropolitan areas with small local authorities, is arguably best placed to make decisions around specialist vocational facilities, employer and higher education engagement strategies. It would also be logical for regional government to oversee the funding of general FE colleges and larger work-based learning providers, who often play a sub-regional or regional role. The concept of a regional layer in the planning of 14–19 learning was supported by the National Audit Office (2007). This would leave local authorities, working on a smaller scale, to co-ordinate the planning of provision in the locality, to oversee funding and admission arrangements for schools and sixth form colleges, and to assist with the development and operation of area-based accountability arrangements. Local school-college consortia, as they do now, would have to be given the power to make day-to-day decisions on collaborative working to meet learner choices and to aid progression. The individual institution would remain the centre of a local learning system, but would need to see itself as part of a 'local ecology', recognizing that its decisions affect the 'health' of other providers in the area and the overall opportunities offered to learners.

A devolved social partnership approach

If an enriched curriculum and enhanced progression opportunities are central aims of a reformed 14–19 phase, engaging a range of social partners becomes an essential strategy. In this section we focus, in particular, on the role of employers because, as we explained in Chapter 5, they are key to improving vocational learning. However, the current government approach is weak – it accords employers a privileged voice in policy-making, it exhorts them to engage with a whole range of activities but has few means of requiring them to play a full part in the education and training system. Here, we suggest a new approach to both employers and to other important social partners at the national, regional and local levels.

Presently, vocational learning is being used to compensate for the alienating effects of a selective general education by providing places for disaffected young people. Proposals for a more inclusive, innovative and practical general education would go some way to preventing this. Employers would then be able to focus on their contribution to the provision and recognition of strongly vocational learning. In this way, a reformed system would make strategic, limited but positive demands of employers rather than asking them to do everything for everybody.

Incentives too would be important for the engagement of social partners. Too much money is currently spent on examinations. These resources could be diverted into joint projects between the different social partners to create what might be termed 'real life education' and to focus on achievement and progression in its widest sense. For example, the Extended Project would be an ideal vehicle for collaborative activity between learners, teachers, community bodies, cultural organizations, higher education providers and employers. Small- and medium-sized enterprises would need business support to enable them to play an active part in education and their engagement could also be publicly recognized through kite-marking and awards. One consequence of this would mean a strengthening of the role of Education Business Partnerships, whose fortunes have waxed and waned according to shifts in policy and resources.

The concept of social partnership suggests a level of obligation that binds the partners together. Here we see a role for increased regulation of the youth labour market through, for example, licence to practise, in which employers and unions jointly set the standards for the social partners in a particular sector. This has been done successfully in the area of health care (Finlay et al. 2007). Learners and employees know what is required of them; employers know what they have to recognize and schools, colleges and work-based learning providers know what they have to offer. Licence to practise thus creates a framework of agreement, common action and predictability in terms of demand for skills and wage returns (Coffield et al. 2008). The public sector could play a leading role here.

Finally, a more devolved approach to governance with greater powers being given to regions and localities would provide new opportunities for engaging with all the social partners. The regional tier, in particular, offers opportunities to bring together large employers (private and public), higher education institutions and civil society organizations. The local level could see smaller-scale collaborations involving smaller enterprises, specialist independent learning providers, community organizations and education institutions facilitated and led by local authorities. Taken together, these measures constitute what we have termed elsewhere a 'devolved social partnership approach' (Spours et al. 2007b), which forms an integral part of a unified 14–19 education and training system.

A radical but gradual reform process

The effective reform of the 14–19 phase is not just about the content of policy but also about how policy is conducted. A more open, inclusive and deliberative policy process would lead to better policy-making by affording spaces in which the different social partners could actively participate. It would also make policy easier to implement. An interviewee outside the world of education providers commented:

> My impression of the school and college system is that there is an overload of change ... because actually when push comes to shove it's about the quality of delivery, it's about people being able to do a good job with the students they've got in front of them and that's very difficult when they're having to take on new initiatives all the time. (PA 2)

The recent history of 14–19 reform under New Labour has been one of deliberate ambiguity – incrementally changing the system but without a clear end-point while, at the same time, discouraging debate. What many of our interviewees were asking for, however, was a clearer vision of where the system was heading, a more explicit set of educational principles for the 14–19 phase as a whole, and a slower and more participative reform process:

> If people are to invest their time and energy and commitment towards something, they need to know its going somewhere and why they're doing it. So, you know, you might walk a mile if you knew where you were going, but if I ask you to walk a mile over rough terrain and I can't tell you where you're going and why you're going there, you're going to be less likely to do it. (PA 10)

Within these overall principles, we recognize that some aspects of reform are more difficult than others. For example, the contentious area of A Levels would require a measured but resolute approach. This would mean balancing proposals for the reform of A Levels, which have been articulated for more than two decades, with the preservation of their inherent strengths. One interviewee suggested a way forward:

> *Actually what Balls [Secretary of State DCSF] ought to do is to say 'We intend to move towards a single qualification. This is the timeline.' There are very many strengths inside A Levels and GCSEs, in terms of the specifications and content. You don't throw the baby out with the bathwater, but you have a look at the idea of how you put it together in an overarching diploma. (PA 11)*

Such a strategy for change would build on strengths, minimise the risk to learners, allow a planned approach to implementation and staff development and reassure parents and other key stakeholders. At the same time, it would be a decisive step towards reshaping 14–19 education in England. It would signal that broad and flexible diploma programmes would replace individual qualifications for all 14–19-year-olds. In Figure 7.4 we illustrate the range of additional initial steps that would need to be taken to bring all forms of learning within an English Diploma system.

CONCLUSION

Radical change of the type we have outlined in this chapter requires a gradual and co-ordinated reform process within a clearly articulated vision. All parts of the system would have to inch forward slowly together so that they created an effective synergy rather than the policy tensions currently witnessed. The calibration of policy, as we have shown in this book, goes much wider than curriculum and qualifications. The reform process would have to be supported by changes to organization and governance, funding, accountability systems and the relationship between education and employment.

An important aspect of connective, reflective and inclusive policy-making is the ability of the system at all levels to learn from the past, from international comparisons, from research and from current experience. This is possible within the scenario of a clear end goal and steps and stages of reform, because these provide the framework for evaluation, deliberation and participation. As one of our interviewees remarked, 'using the curriculum and qualifications strategy as a sort of political football is a huge problem' (PA 22). What is needed is a cross-party dialogue and the involvement of all social partners in the creation of a 14–19 phase that is not only more inclusive and more effective, but that articulates with the phases that precede and follow it.

- Declare a timeline for the introduction of an open/general English Diploma at four levels – Entry to Advanced.
- Bring the 17 lines of Diplomas, BTEC Diplomas and other vocational awards into the wider English Diploma System.
- Re-engineer GCSEs and A Levels to form components of a suite of open/general English Diplomas.
- Integrate the Foundation Learning Tier into the Entry and Level 1 English Diplomas.
- Employ the credit system developed for adults across the 14–19 English Diploma System, balanced with rules of combination to ensure coherent learner programmes.
- Develop and extend Generic Learning to become the Common Core for all English Diplomas.
- Create a major development programme around the Extended Project because of its ability to offer personalization, skill development and the involvement of different social partners.
- Experiment with new professional forms of assessment around the Extended Project using the concept of chartered examiners.
- Develop strong systems of information, advice and guidance as part of a comprehensive focus on progression in a local/regional area.
- Move to area-based accountability and funding systems to aid collaboration and local innovation around the stages of English Diploma development.
- Strengthen Education Business Partnerships and other fora for the discussion of area-wide agreements with social partners in the locality.

Figure 7.4 *Initial steps towards a more unified system*

Given the contentious and fragile nature of the 14–19 phase, we advocate a far more open process of discussion to find common ground for a more permanent settlement, in which 14–19 education and training is able to play its unique and important role in the creation of an effective lifelong learning system.

We do not expect immediate consensus and we certainly do not expect everyone to agree with some of the perspectives offered in this book. However, we are confident that a more open and deliberative policy process would create the basis for a more enduring 14–19 phase in which educational argument would have the chance to shape the future.

references

Adnett, N. and Davies, P. (2003) Schooling reforms in England: from quasi-markets to co-operation. Journal of Education Policy, 18 (4), 393–406.

Adult Learning Inspectorate (ALI) (2006) *The Final Annual Report of the Chief Inspector*. Coventry: ALI.

Aiston, S., Rudd, P. and O'Donnell, L. (2002) *School partnerships in action: A case study of West Sussex specialist schools*. Slough: NFER.

Ashton, D. (2006) *Lessons from abroad* SSDA Catalyst Issue 2. Wath-upon-Dearne: SSDA.

Ashton, D. and Green, F. (1996) *Education, training and the global economy*. Cheltenham: Elgar.

Association of Colleges (AoC) (2002) *Response to 14–19 Green Paper*. London: AoC.

AoC, ATL, GSA, HMC, NAHT, NASUWT, NATFHE, NUT, PAT, SHA, SHMHIS (1997) *Key principles for curriculum and qualification reform from 14+*. London: Institute of Education.

Association of Teachers and Lecturers (ATL) (2002) *14–19: extending opportunities, raising standards: ATL's response to the Green Paper*. London: ATL.

Atkinson, M., Springate, I., Johnson, F. and Halsey, K. (2007) *Inter-school collaboration: a literature review*. Slough: NFER.

Audit Commission (1998) *A fruitful partnership: Effective partnership working*. London: Audit Commission.

Baker, M. (2005) 'Why Tomlinson was turned down'. *BBC News 24*, 26 Feb.

Ball, S. J. (2007) *Education plc: understanding private sector participation on public sector education*. London: Routledge.

Ball, S. J. , Maguire, M. and Macrae, S. (2000) '"Worlds apart" – education markets in the post-16 sector in one urban locale 1995–98' in Coffield, F. (ed.) *Differing visions of the Learning Society*. Bristol: The Policy Press.

Bates, I. (1997) *Problematizing 'empowerment' in education and work: an exploration of the GNVQ*. Occasional Paper No. 7, School of Education, University of Leeds.

Bates, I. and Riseborough, G. (1993) 'Deepening divisions, fading solutions' in Bates, I. and Riseborough, G. (eds) *Youth and inequality*. Buckingham: Open University Press.

Bathmaker, A-M. (2001) 'It's the perfect education': Lifelong learning and the experience of Foundation-level GNVQ student. *Journal of Vocational Education and Training*, 53 (1), 81–100.

Beaumont, G. (1996) *Review of 100 NVQs and SVQs: A report submitted to the DfEE*. London: DfEE.

Bentley, T. (1998) *Learning beyond the classroom: education for a changing world*. London: Routledge.

Billett, S. (2004) 'Learning in the workplace: reappraisals and reconceptions' in Hayward, G. and James, S. (eds) *Balancing the skills equation: Key issues and challenges for policy and practice*. Bristol: The Policy Press.

Blair, T. (Rt Hon.) (2004) *Speech to the CBI manufacturing annual dinner*, 18 Oct.

Blatchford, P. (1996) Pupils' views on schoolwork and school from 7–16 years. *Research Papers in Education*, 11 (3) 263–288.

Boyd. S. (2002) *Partnership working: European social partnership models*. Glasgow: STUC.

Briggs, A., Hall, I., Mercer, D., Smith, F., Swann, T. and Falzon, C. (2007) *Leading partnerships for 14–19 education provision*. Centre for Excellence in Leadership, University of Newcastle. www.ncl.ac.uk/ecls/research/project/1918, accessed 8 Nov. 2007.

British Broadcasting Corporation (BBC) News (2004a) *Exam shake-up for secondary schools*. 18 Oct.

BBC News (2004b) *Mike Tomlinson: An interview with Jeremy Paxman*. 18 Feb.

BBC (2006) *Harder A-Levels and boost for IB*. 30 Nov. 2006. http://news.bbc.co.uk/1/hi/education/6159857.stm, accessed 30 Jan. 2008.

BBC (2007a) *Diplomas 'may go horribly wrong.'* 9 Mar. (http://news.bbc.co/1/hi/education/6435563.stm), accessed 13 Aug. 2007.

BBC (2007b) *Universities have Diploma doubts*. 27 July. (http://news.bbc.co/1/hi/education/6917842.stm), accessed 13 Aug. 2007.

Brown, P., Green, A. and Lauder, H. (eds) (2001) *High skills: Globalisation, competitiveness and skill formation*. Oxford: Oxford University Press.

Capey, J. (1995) *GNVQ assessment review*. London: National Council for

Vocational Qualifications.

Centre for Lifelong Learning (CLL) (2007) *An evaluation of the functional skills trials.* Warwick: University of Warwick.

Chitty, C. (1991) 'Towards new definitions of vocationalism' in Chitty, C. (ed.) *Post-16 education: Studies in access and achievement.* London: Kogan Page.

Clare, J. (2004) Diplomas to replace GCSE and A Levels. *Daily Telegraph,* 18 Feb. 2004.

Clarke, L. (2007) 'The emergence and reinforcement of class and gender divisions through vocational education in England' in Clarke, L. and Winch, C. (eds) *Vocational education: International approaches, developments and systems.* London: Routledge.

Clarke, L. and Winch, C. (eds) (2007) *Vocational education: International approaches, developments and systems.* London: Routledge.

Cockett, M. (1996) 'Vocationalism and vocational courses 14–16' in Cockett, M. and Callaghan, J. (eds) *Education and training 14–19: Chaos or coherence?* London: David Fulton.

Coffield, F., Edward, S., Finlay, I., Hodgson, A., Steer, R. and Spours, K. (2008) *Improving learning, skills and inclusion: The impact of policy on post-compulsory education.* London: Routledge/Falmer.

Coles, J. (2006) *The recent announcement on the International Baccalaureate, Letter to local authorities, 5 Dec 2006.* London: DfES.

Colley, H. (2006) Learning to labour with feeling: class, gender and emotion in childcare education and training. *Contemporary Issues in Early Childhood,* 7 (1) 15–29.

CBI (2007) *Shaping up for the future: The business vision for education and skills.* London: CBI.

Coopers and Lybrand (1985) *A challenge to complacency.* Sheffield: MSC.

Crombie-White, R., Pring, R., Brockington, D. (1995) *14–19 education and training: Implementing a unified system of learning.* London: Royal Society of Arts.

Curtis, P. (2004) Diploma set to end 60-year exam system. *Guardian Unlimited,* 18 Oct.

Curtis, P. (2005) Teachers reject White Paper proposals. *Guardian Unlimited,* 23 Feb.

Daily Mail (2004) Comment, Failed exams. *Daily Mail,* 16 Feb.

Dale, R. (1990) *The TVEI story: Policy, practice and preparation for the workforce.* Milton Keynes: Open University Press.

De Pear, S. (1997) Excluded pupils' views of their educational needs and experience. *Support for Learning,* 12 (2), 19–22.

Dearing, Sir R. (1996) *Review of qualifications for 16–19 year olds*. London: SCAA.

Department of Education Northern Ireland (DENI) (2007) 14–19 policy. www.deni.gov.uk/index/80curriculumandassessment_pg/22-curriculum_and_assessment-14–19_policy.htm, accessed 21 Dec. 2007.

Department for Education/Employment Department/Welsh Office (1991) *Education and training for the 21st century*. London: HMSO.

Department for Education and Employment (DfEE) (1996) *Learning to compete: education and training for 14–19 year olds*. London: Stationary Office.

DfEE (1999) *Learning to succeed: A new framework for post-16 learning*. London: DfEE.

DfEE/DENI/WO (1997) *Qualifying for success: A consultation paper on the future of post-16 qualifications*. London: DfEE

Department of Children, Schools and Families (DCSF) (2007a) *Raising the participation age – four building blocks*. Speech to the Fabian Society, Institute of Education, University of London, 5 Nov.

DCSF (2007b) *Confidence in standards: Regulating and developing qualifications and assessment*. London: DCSF.

DCFS (2007c) *Changes to A Levels*. www.dfes.gov.uk/14–19/index.cfm?sid=3&pid=233&ctype=None&ptype=Contents, accessed 20 Sept. 2007.

DCFS (2007d) *Getting the basics right: Generic definition of functional skills*. www.dfes.gov.uk/14–19/index.cfm?sid=3&pid=225&lid=188&ctype=Text&ptype=Single, accessed 20 Sept. 2007.

DCSF (2007e) *Foundation Learning Tier*. www.dfes.gov.uk/14–19/index.cfm?sid=3&pid=227&ctype, accessed 20 Sept. 2007.

DCSF (2007f) *Diplomas could become qualification of choice for young people*. DCSF Press release 2007/0195, 23 Oct.

DCSF (2007g) *Every Child Matters: Change for children*. www.everychildmatters.gov.uk/aims, accessed 9 Nov. 2007.

DCFS (2007h) *September Guarantee guidance*. www.dfes.gov.uk/localauthorities/index.cfm?action=content&contentID=8363, accessed 6 Nov. 2007.

Department for Education and Skills (DfES) (2001a) *Schools achieving success*. London: DFES.

DfES (2001b) *Far-reaching reform to put the pupil first and enable every school to succeed*. DfES Press Release, 5 Sept.

DfES (2002) *14–19 education: Extending opportunities, raising standards*. London: Stationery Office.

DfES (2003) *14–19 excellence and opportunity: Government response to the*

14–19 Green Paper. London: DfES.

DfES (2005a) *14–19 education and skills.* London: DfES.

DfES (2005b) *14–19 implementation plan.* London: DfES.

DfES (2005c) *Higher standards, better schools for all.* Norwich: Stationery Office.

DfES (2006a) *Youth matters: Next steps, something to do, somewhere to go, someone to talk to.* Annersley: DfES.

DfES (2006b) *Diploma champions to drive forward reform of the 14–19 agenda,* DfES Press Release. 12 Dec.

DfES (2006c) *The specialised diploma gateway.* London: DfES.

DfES (2006d) *Specialised diplomas – your questions answered.* www.dfes.gov.uk/14-19/documents/DfESDiplomasJuly06.pdf, accessed 20 Sept. 2006.

DfES (2006e) *Further education: Raising skills, improving life chances.* London: DfES.

DfES (2007a) *Participation in education, training and employment by 16–18 year olds in England: 2005 and 2006 and participation in education by 16 and 17 year olds in each local area in England: 2004 and 2005,* Statistical first release 22/2007. London: DfES.

DfES (2007b) *Statistical first release 01/200, GCSE and equivalent examination results in England, 2005/06.* 10 Jan. London: DfES.

DfES (2007c) *Statistical first release 02/2007, GCE/VCE A/AS and equivalent examination results in England 2005/6.* London: DfES.

DfES (2007d) *Raising expectations: staying on in education and training post-16.* London: DfES.

Department of Education and Science (DES) (1988) *Advancing A Levels: Report of the committee chaired by Professor Higginson.* London: HMSO.

Department of Employment (DoE) (1988) *Employment for the 1990s.* London: HMSO.

Department for Innovation, Universities and Skills (DIUS) (2007) *World class skills: Implementing the Leitch Review of Skills in England.* London: HM Government.

DIUS/DCSF (2008) *World class apprenticeships: Unlocking talent, building skills for all.* London: DIUS/DCSF

Ecclestone, K. (2002) *Learning autonomy in post-compulsory education: The politics and practice of formative assessment.* London: Routledge/Falmer.

Ecclestone, K. (2006) *Assessment in post-compulsory education: Paper 2: commitment and comfort zones: purposes and practices of formative assessment in post-16 programmes.* Paper presented to the British Educational Research Association, University of Warwick, 6–9 Sept.

Ecclestone, K. (2007) Commitment, compliance and comfort zones: the effects of formative assessment on vocational education and students' learning careers, *Assessment in Education*, 14 (3), 315–333.

Edge Foundation (2007) *What teachers and further education lecturers think about the Diplomas*. London: Anderson Associates.

Evans, B. (1992) *The politics of the training market: From the Manpower Services Commission to Training and Enterprise Councils*. New York: Routledge.

Finlay, I., Hodgson, A. and Steer, R. (2007) Flowers in the desert: the impact of policy on basic skills provision in the workplace. *Journal of Vocational Education and Training*, 59 (2), 231–248.

Further Education Development Agency/Institute of Education/Nuffield (1997) General National Vocational Qualifications in the further education sector in England. National survey report. London: FEDA.

Financial Times (2004) A for effort but C for detail. *Financial Times*, 18 Feb.

Finegold, D. and Soskice, D. (1988) The failure of training in Britain: Analysis and prescription. *Oxford Review of Economic Policy*, 4 (3), 21–53.

Finegold, D., Keep, E., Miliband, D., Raffe, D., Spours, K. and Young, M. (1990) *A British Baccalaureate: Overcoming divisions between education and training*. London: IPPR.

Fisher, L. (2007) Pedagogy and the Curriculum 2000 reforms at post-16: The 'learn it, forget it' culture? *The Curriculum Journal*, 18 (1), 103–114.

Flint, C. (2004) A long awaited revolution. *Adults Learning*, 16 (4), 16–18.

Frost, D. (2007) *New League show 'shocking truth' about lack of basic skills*. British Chambers of Commerce News Release. 10 Jan. www.chamberonline.co.uk/YXMg-ZNoarMi4g.html, accessed 20 Sept. 2007.

Frye, M. and Webb, A. (2002) *Working together: Effective partnership working from the ground*. London: HM Treasury.

Fuller. A. (2004) *Expecting too much? Modern Apprenticeship: purposes, participation and attainment*. Nuffield 14–19 Review Working Paper No. 10 www.nuffield14-19review.org.uk/cgi/documents/documents.cgi?a=17&t=template.htm, accessed 1 Oct. 2007.

Fuller, A. and Unwin, L. (2003) Creating a 'Modern Apprenticeship': a critique of the UK's multi-sector, social inclusion approach. *Journal of Education and Work*, 16 (1), 5–25.

Fuller, A. and Unwin, L. (2007) *Conceptualising and identifying 'good' practice in contemporary apprenticeships: The struggle for coherence in a complex economic and educational landscape*. Paper presented to the Annual Conference of the British Educational Research Association, Institute of Education, London, 3–5 Sep.

Gardner, S. (2007) *Listening to the voice of GCE A level students and their teachers*. Nuffield 14–19 Review Working Paper No. 43. www. nuffield14–19review.org.uk/cgi/documents, accessed 16 Oct. 2007.

Gleeson, D. and Keep, E. (2004) Voice without accountability: the changing relationship between employers, the state and education. *Oxford Review of Education*, 30 (1), 37–63.

Golden, S., Nelson, J., O'Donnell, L. and Morris, M. (2004) *Evaluation of Increased Flexibility of 14–16 year olds Programme: The first year*. DfES Research Report RR511. Nottingham: DfES.

Golden, S., O'Donnell, L. and Rudd, P. (2005) *Evaluation of Increased Flexibility for 14–16 Year Olds Programme: The second year*. RR609. Nottingham: DfES.

Grainger, P., Hodgson, A. and Spours, K. (2007) 'A pan-London approach to 14–19 learning: a figment of the imagination or a potential reality?', in Brighouse, T. and Fullick, L. (eds) *Education in a Global City Essays*. London Bedford Way Paper 32, Institute of Education, University of London.

Gray, J., Jesson, D. and Tranmer, M. (1993) *Boosting full-time participation in post-16 education: A study of some key factors in England and Wales*, Youth Cohort Study No. 20. Sheffield: Employment Department.

Green, A. (1991) 'Comprehensive education and training: possibilities and prospects' in Chitty, C. (ed.) *Post-16 education: Studies in access and achievement*. London: Kogan Page.

Green, A. (1998) Core skills, key skills and general culture: in search of the common foundation in vocational education. *Evaluation and Research in Education*, 12 (1), 23–43.

Green, A. (2006) Models of lifelong learning and the 'knowledge society'. *Compare*, 36 (3), 307–325.

Green, A. and Lucas, N. (eds) (1999) *FE and lifelong learning: Realigning the sector for the 21st century*. London: Bedford Way Papers, Institute of Education, University of London.

Green, A. and Steedman, H. (1993) *Educational provision, educational attainment and the needs of industry: A review of the research for Germany, France, Japan, the USA and Britain Report Series 5*. London: National Institute of Economic and Social Research.

Green, A., Wolf, A. and Leney, T. (1999) *Convergence and divergence in European education systems*. London: Bedford Way Papers, Institute of Education, University of London.

Greenwood, M., Tait, T., Anderson, M., Smith, D., Collins, C. and Monoz, S. (2007) *Research to examine the experience of providers in delivering and assessing key skills and adult skills in literacy and numeracy in order to inform the development and implementation of the functional skills qualifications.* London: LSN.

Haines, G. (2006) *Vocational courses in the Key Stage 4 curriculum – A national survey of secondary headteachers' views and experiences.* Paper presented to the Annual Conference of the British Educational Research Association, University of Warwick, 3–5 Sept.

Hall, S. (2003) New Labour's Double Shuffle, *Soundings.* www.lwbooks.co.uk/journals/articles/nov03.html, accessed 9 July 2007.

Hargreaves, D. (2001a) *Review of Curriculum 2000 – QCA's report on phase 1.* London: QCA.

Hargreaves, D. (2001b) *Review of Curriculum 2000 – QCA's report on phase 2.* London: QCA.

Harland, J. (1991) 'Upper secondary education in England and Wales: An overview of curriculum pathways' in Chitty, C. (ed.) *Post-16 education: Studies in access and achievement.* London: Kogan Page.

Hayes, J. and Kelly, S. (2007) *Towards a gold standards for craft: Guaranteeing professional apprenticeships.* London: Centre for Policy Studies.

Hayward, G. and James, S. (eds) (2004) *Balancing the skills equation: Key issues and challenges for policy and practice.* Bristol: The Policy Press.

Hayward, G., Hodgson, A., Johnson, J., Oancea, A., Pring, R., Spours, K., Wright, S. and Wilde, S. (2005) *Annual report of the Nuffield 14–19 Review 2004–5.* OUDES: University of Oxford

Hayward, G., Hodgson, A., Johnson, J., Oancea, A., Pring, R., Spours, K., Wilde, S. and Wright, S. (2006) *Annual Report of the Nuffield 14–19 Review 2005–6.* OUDES: University of Oxford.

Higham, J. (2003) *Continuity and discontinuity in the '14–19 Curriculum'.* Nuffield 14–19 Review Working Paper No. 4. www.nuffield14–19review.org.uk/cgi/documents) accessed 16 Oct. 2007.

Higham, J. and Yeomans, D. (2005) *Collaborative approaches to 14–19 education and training provision.* Discussion Paper for Nuffield Review of 14–19 Education and Training presented at the Nuffield Foundation on 17 May 2005. www.nuffield14–19review.org.uk/documents.shtml, accessed 16 Oct. 2007.

Higham, J. and Yeomans, D. (2006) *Emerging provision and practice in 14–19 education and training. A report on the evaluation of the third year of the 14–19 Pathfinder Initiative.* DfES Research Report RR737. Nottingham: DfES.

Higham, J. and Yeomans, D. (2007a) 'Policy memory and policy amnesia in 14–19 education: Learning from the past?' in Raffe, D. and Spours, K. (eds) *Policy-making and policy learning in 14–19 education.* Bedford Way Paper No 26. London: Institute of Education.

Higham, J. and Yeomans, D. (2007b) Curriculum choice, flexibility and differentiation 14–19: the way forward or flawed prospectus. *London Review of Education*, 5 (3), 281–298.

Higham, J., Haynes, G., Wragg, C. and Yeomans, D. (2004) *14–19 Pathfinders: An evaluation of the first year*. London: DFES.

Higham, J., Sharp, P. and Yeomans. D. (1996) *The emerging 16–19 curriculum: Policy and provision*. London: David Fulton.

Hill, I. (2003) 'The International Baccalaureate' in Phillips, G. and Pound, T. (eds) *The Baccalaureate: A model for curriculum reform*. London: Kogan Page.

Hodgson, A. and Spours, K. (1997a) 'From the 1991 White Paper to the Dearing Report: a conceptual and historical framework for the 1990s' in Hodgson, A. and Spours, K. (eds) *Dearing and Beyond: 14–19 curriculum, qualifications and frameworks*. London: Kogan Page.

Hodgson, A. and Spours, K. (eds) (1997b) *Dearing and beyond: 14–19 qualifications, frameworks and systems*. London: Kogan Page.

Hodgson, A. and Spours, K. (1999) *New Labour's educational agenda: Issues and policies for education and training from 14+*. London: Kogan Page.

Hodgson, A. and Spours, K. (2000) Expanding higher education in the UK: from 'system slowdown' to 'system acceleration'. *Higher Education Quarterly*, 54 (4), 295–322.

Hodgson, A. and Spours, K. (2001) Part-time work and full-time education in the UK: the emergence of a curriculum and policy issues. *Journal of Education and Work*, 14 (3), 373–388.

Hodgson, A. and Spours, K. (2002) Key skills for all? The key skills qualification and Curriculum 2000. *Journal of Education Policy*, 17 (1), 22–47.

Hodgson, A. and Spours, K. (2003) *Beyond A Levels: Curriculum 2000 and the reform of 14–19 qualifications*. London: Kogan Page.

Hodgson, A. and Spours, K. (2006a) The organisation of 14–19 education and training in England: beyond weakly collaborative arrangements. *Journal of Education and Work*, 19 (4), 325–342.

Hodgson, A. and Spours, K. (2006b) An analytical framework for policy engagement: the contested case of 14–19 reform in England. *Journal of Education Policy*, 21 (6), 679–696.

Hodgson, A., Spours, K. and Waring, M. (2005a) Higher education, Curriculum 2000 and the future reform of 14–19 qualifications in England. *Oxford Review of Education*, 31 (4), 479–495.

Hodgson, A., Spours, K., Coffield, F., Steer, R., Finlay, I., Edward, S. and Gregson, M. (2005b) *A new learning and skills landscape? The LSC within the LSS*. ESRC TLRP Project Research Report 1. London: Institute of

Education, University of London.

Hodgson, A. Spours, K. and Wilson, P. (2006) *Tomlinson and the Framework for Achievement: A unified answer to a divided system.* Leicester: NIACE.

Hodgson, A., Spours, K., Steer, R., Coffield, F., Finlay, I. and Gregson, M. (2007) *A seismic shift? Policy perspectives on the changing learning and skills landscape.* ESRC TLRP Project Research Report 5. London: Institute of Education, University of London.

Hodkinson, P. (1996) 'Careership: the individual, choice and markets in the transition into work' in Avis, J., Bloomer, M. Esland, G., Gleeson, D. and Hodkinson, P. (eds) *Knowledge and Nationhood.* London: Cassell.

House of Commons Education and Skills Committee (HoC) (2007) *14–19 Diplomas: Fifth report of session 2006–07,* HC249. London: The Stationery Office.

House of Lords, Select Committee on Economic Affairs (2007) *Apprenticeship: A key route to skill. Volume 1: report.* London: The Stationery Office.

Howieson, C., Raffe, D., Spours, K. and Young, M. (1997) Unifying academic and vocational learning: the state of the debate in England and Scotland. *Journal of Education and Work,* 10 (1), 5–35.

Huddleston, P., Keep, E. and Unwin, L. (2005) *What might the Tomlinson and White Paper proposals mean for vocational education and work-based learning.* Nuffield 14–19 Review Discussion Paper 33. www.nuffield14–19review.org.uk, accessed Oct. 2007.

Hyland, T. (1994) *Competence, education and NVQs: Dissenting perspectives.* London: Cassell.

Independent (2007) A good plan scuppered by political cowardice, *Independent,* 13 Aug. 2007.

Independent Schools Council (ISC) (2003) *Good neighbours. ISC schools and their local communities.* London: ISC.

Institute of Directors (IOD) (2007) *Education briefing book 2007.* London: IOD.

Institute of Manpower Studies (1984) *Competence and competition: Training and education in the Federal Republic of Germany, the United States and Japan.* London: NEDC/MSC.

Johnson, A. (Rt Hon.) (2006) *Creating a confident nation for a changing world.* Speech to the Association of Colleges, 21 Nov. www.dfes.gov.uk/speeches/search_detail.cfm?ID=435, accessed 30 Jan. 2008.

Joint Council for Qualifications (JCQ) (2007a) *Improvements in results for English, mathematics and science at GCSE.* News Release. 23 Aug. www.jcq.org.uk/attachments/published/394/GCSEpressrelease2007.pdf, accessed 20 Sep. 2007.

JCQ (2007b) *Entry trends 2007 – GCSE, Applied GCSE and Entry Level.* www.jcq.org.uk/attachments/published/396/GCSE~AppGCSE~Entry %20Trends.pdf, accessed 20 Sep. 2007.

JCQ (2007c) *Entry trends 2007 – A, AS, AEA tables.* www.jcq.org.uk/attach-ments/published/387/Appendix%20Entry%20Trends~Final%20version. pdf, accessed 20 Sep. 2007.

JCQ (2007d) *Improvement in A Level results and increased entries in maths, science and modern foreign languages.* News Release. 16 Oct. www.jcq.org.uk/ attachments/published/386/A%20level%20News%20release%20FINAL .pdf, accessed 20 Sep. 2007.

Kearns, J. (2004) 'Challenges at the chalkface: one school's experience of the Baccalaureate' in Ryan, C. (ed.) *Bac or basics: Challenges for the 14–19 curriculum.* London: Social Market Foundation.

Keep, E. (2005a) Reflections on the curious absence of employers, labour market incentives and labour market regulation in English 14–19 policy: first signs of a change of direction? *Journal of Education Policy,* 20 (5), 533–553.

Keep, E. (2005b) *The future of the work-based route in England – the tethered beetle of policy takes another turn.* Lecture given as part of the Institute of Education Open Lecture Series, Mar. 2005.

Keep, E. and Mayhew, K. (1998) *Was Ratner right? Product market and competitive strategies and their links with skills and knowledge.* London: Employment Policy Institute.

Keep, E. and Payne, J. (2004) '"I can't believe it's not skill": the changing meaning of skill in the UK context and some implications' in Hayward, G. and James, S. (eds) *Balancing the skills equation: Key issues and challenges for policy and practice.* Bristol: The Policy Press.

Labour Party (1992) *Opening doors.* London: Labour Party.

Labour Party (1996) *Aiming higher: Labour's proposals for the reform of the 14–19 curriculum.* London: Labour Party.

Labour Party (1997) *Because Britain deserves better: Labour Party Manifesto.* London: Labour Party. www.labour-party.org.uk/manifestos/1997/1997-labour-manifesto.shtml, accessed 20 Sep. 2007.

Lauder, H. (2001) 'Innovation, skill diffusion and social exclusion' in Brown, P., Green, A. and Lauder, H. (eds) *High skills: Globalisation, competitiveness and skill formation.* Oxford: Oxford University Press.

Le Metais, J. (2002) *International developments in upper secondary education: Context, provision and issues,* INCA thematic study No 8. Slough: NFER.

Learning and Skills Council (LSC) (2005) *Level 2 entitlement: Guide for providers, stakeholders and intermediaries.* Coventry: LSC. http://readingroom.lsc.gov.uk/lsc/2005/learningopportunities/adults/level-2-entitlement-guide-for-providers-stakeholders.pdf, accessed 20 Sep. 2007.

LSC (2006a) *Delivering learning and skills: Progress report 2006.* Coventry: LSC.

LSC (2006b) *Employer perceptions of migrant workers: Research report.* Coventry: LSC.

LSC (2006c) *e2e: A simple fact sheet on Entry to Employment: Issue 5.* Coventry: LSC.

LSC (2006d) *National learner satisfaction survey, highlights from 2004–5.* Coventry: LSC.

LSC (2007) Further education and work-based learning for young people – learner outcomes in England 2005/6. *LSC statistical first release,* 17 Apr.

Leitch S. (2006) *Prosperity for all in the global economy – world class skills.* London: HMT.

Lipsett, A. (2007) New Diploma tariffs may outstrip A Levels. *Guardian Online,* 19 Dec. http://politics.guardian.co.uk/publicservices/story/0,,2229683,00.html, accessed 21 Dec. 2007.

London Skills and Employment Board (LSEB) (2007) *Skills and employment in London: Proposals for the London Skills and Employment Board's strategy.* London: LSEB.

Lucas, G. (2008) *The 14–19 curriculum and qualifications: Options in independent schools.* Nuffield 14–19 Review discussion paper. www.nuffield14-19review.org.uk/, accessed 4 Feb. 2008.

Lumby, J. and Foskett, N. (2005) *14–19 education: Policy, leadership and learning.* London: Sage.

Lumby, J. and Foskett, N. (2007) 'Turbulence masquerading as change: exploring 14–19 policy' in Raffe, D. and Spours, K. (eds) *Policy-making and policy learning in 14–19 education.* London: Institute of Education, University of London Bedford Way papers.

Lumby, J. and Morrison, M. (2006) Partnership, conflict and gaming. *Journal of Education Policy,* 21 (3), 223–242.

Machin, S. and Vignoles, A. (2006) *Education policy in the UK.* London: Centre for the Economics of Education, London School of Economics. http://cep.lse.ac.uk/research/skills/skillsforall.asp, accessed 30 Nov. 2007.

Macintosh, S. (2004) The impact of vocational qualifications on the labour market: outcomes of low achieving school-leavers. http://cep.lse.ac.uk/research/skills/skillsforall.asp, accessed 30 Nov. 2007.

McIntosh, S. (2007) *A cost-benefit analysis of apprenticeships and other vocational qualifications.* DfES research report RR834. Nottingham: DfES.

Macleod, D. and Hughes, M. (2005) *What we know about working with employers: A synthesis of LSDA work on employer engagement.* London: LSDA.

Mansell, J. (1991) 'The role of the further education sector in post-16 education' in Chitty, C. (ed.) *Post-16 education: Studies in access and achievement.* London: Kogan Page.

Morris, E. (Rt Hon.) (2002) 'Foreword' in DfES *14–19 Education: Extending opportunities, raising standards.* London: DfES.

Munday, F. and Fawcett, B. (2002) *Models of 16–19 collaboration. A report for Oxfordshire Learning Partnership.* Oxford: Oxfordshire Learning Partnership.

National Advisory Council for Education and Training Targets (NACETT) (1994) *Review of the national targets for education and training: Proposals for consultation.* London: NACETT.

National Association of Headteachers (NAHT) (1987) *14–18 action plan.* NAHT: Haywards Heath.

National Audit Office (NAO) (2005) *Employers' perspectives on improving skills for employment.* London: The Stationery Office.

NAO (2007) *Partnering for success: Preparing to deliver the 14–19 education reforms in England.* London: The Stationery Office.

National Commission on Education (NCE) (1995) *Learning to succeed: The way ahead.* London: NCE.

National Skills Taskforce (2000) *Skills for all: Proposals for a national skills agenda.* London: DfEE.

National Union of Teachers (NUT) (1995) *14–19 strategy for the future: The road to equality.* London: NUT.

NUT (2007) *The National Union of Teachers' response to the House of Commons Education and Skills Committee Enquiry into 14–19 Specialised Diplomas.* London: NUT.

Nelson, J., Morris, M., Rickinson, M., Blenkinsop, S. and Spielhofer, T. (2001) *Disapplying National Curriculum subjects to facilitate extended work-related learning at Key Stage 4: An evaluation.* DfES Research Report RR293. Nottingham: DfES.

New Local Government Network (NLGN) (2007) *Redesigning regions.* www.nlgn.org.uk/public/events/redesigning-regions/, accessed 8 Nov. 2007.

Newman, J. (2000) 'Beyond the new public management? Modernising public services' in Clarke, J., Gewirtz, S. and McLoughlin, E. (eds) *New managerialism, new welfare?* London: Sage and Open University Press.

Newman, J. (2001) *Modernising governance: New Labour, policy and society.* London: Sage.

Nuffield 14-19 Review (2007) *The new 14-19 diplomas.* Issue Paper 1. www.nuffield14-19review.org.uk/, accessed 2 Feb. 2008.

Nuffield 14-19 Review (2008a) *Apprenticeship: Prospects for growth.* Issue Paper 3. www.nuffield14-19review.org.uk/, accessed 2 Feb. 2008.

Nuffield 14-19 Review (2008b) The quality of apprenticeship. Issue Paper 4. www.nuffield14-19review.org.uk/, accessed 2 Feb. 2008.

O'Donnell, L., Golden, S., McCrone, T. Rudd, P. and Walker, M. (2006) *Evaluation of the increased flexibility for 14–16 year olds programme: Delivery for cohorts 3 and 4 and the future.* DfES Research Brief No. RB790. London: DfES.

OCR (2006) The Foundation Learning Tier. *Diploma Watch Newsletter* Issue 3, August. Cambridge: OCR.

Office for Standards in Education (Ofsted) (2003a) *Curriculum 2000: Implementation.* HMI 993. London: Ofsted.

Ofsted (2003b) *Supporting 14 to 19 education: Evidence from the work of 12 LEAs.* Ofsted: e-publication. www.ofsted.gov.uk, accessed Feb. 2005.

Ofsted (2004) *Developing new vocational pathways: Final report on the introduction of new GCSEs.* London: Ofsted.

Ofsted (2005) *The Key Stage 4 curriculum: Increased flexibility, work-related learning and Young Apprenticeship Programmes.* London: Ofsted.

Ofsted (2007) *The annual report of Her Majesty's Chief Inspector.* London: Ofsted.

Ofsted/FEFC (1999) *Post-16 collaboration. School sixth forms and the further education sector.* London: FEFC.

Pearce, N. and Hillman, J. (1998) *Wasted youth: Raising achievement and tackling social exclusion.* London: IPPR.

Perry, A. and Simpson, M. (2006) *Delivering quality and choice: How performance indicators help and how performance indicators hinder.* London: LSDA.

Pound, T. (1999) 'From Crowther to Curriculum 2000' in Phillips, G. and Pound, T. (eds) *The Baccalaureate: A model for curriculum reform.* London: Kogan Page.

Prime Minister's Strategy Unit (PMSU) (2006) *The UK government's approach to public service reform.* London: Cabinet Office.

PMSU (2007) *Building on progress: Public services.* London: Cabinet Office.

Principal Learning Ltd (2003) *Illustrations of different local organisational structures for collaborative delivery of post-16 education and training.* London: DfES.

Pring, R. (1995) *Closing the gap: Liberal education and vocational preparation.* London: Hodder and Stoughton.

Pring, R. (2007) '14–19 and lifelong learning: distinguishing between academic and vocational learning' in Clarke, L. and Winch, C. (eds) *Vocational education: International approaches, developments and systems*. London: Routledge.

Qualifications and Curriculum Authority (QCA) (2007a) *Controlled assessment*. London: QCA.

QCA (2007b) *QCA accredits new A Levels from 2008*. www.qca.org.uk/qca_13027.aspx, accessed 20 Sep. 2007.

QCA (2007c) *The Specialised Diploma: Qualification structure*. London: QCA.

QCA (2007d) *Work-related learning at Key Stage 4, first replication study: A QCA-commissioned report on the development of work-related learning in the 3 years since 2004*. London: QCA.

QCA, CCEA, ACCAC (1998) *An overarching certificate at advanced level: Research specification*. London: QCA.

QCA/LSC (2005) *Developing a Foundation Learning Tier: A QCA and LSC initiative*. London: QCA.

QCA/LSC (2007) *Foundation Learning Tier*. London: QCA.

QCA, Welsh Assembly Government (WAG) and CEA (2006) *Draft framework and criteria for the extended project (level 3)*. London: QCA.

Raffe, D. (2006) 'Devolution and divergence in education policy' in Adams, J. and Schmueker, K. (eds) *Devolution in practice 2006: Public policy differences within the UK*. London: IPPR.

Raffe, D. (2007) 'Learning from "home international" comparisons: 14–19 policy across the United Kingdom' in Raffe, D. and Spours, K. (eds) *Policy-making and policy learning in 14–19 education*. London: Institute of Education, University of London Bedford Way Papers.

Raffe, D. and Spours, K. (eds) (2007) *Policy-making and policy learning in 14–19 education*. London: Institute of Education, University of London Bedford Way Papers.

Raffe, D., Howieson, C., Spours, K. and Young, M. (1998) The unification of post-compulsory education: Towards a conceptual framework. *British Journal of Educational Studies*, 46 (2), 169–187.

Raffe, D., Howieson, C. and Tinklin, T. (2007) The impact of a unified curriculum and qualifications system: The Higher Still reform of post-16 education in Scotland. *British Education Research Journal*, 33 (4), 459–478.

Raggatt, P. and Unwin, L. (eds) (1991) *Change and intervention: Vocational education and training*. London: The Falmer Press.

Richardson, W. (1993) 'The 16–19 education and training debate: "deciding factors" in the British public policy process' in Richardson, W., Woolhouse, J. and Finegold, D. (eds) *The reform of post-16 education and training in England and Wales*. London: Longman.

Richardson, W. (2007) Public policy failure and fiasco in education: perspectives on the British examination crises of 2000–2002 and other episodes since 1975. *Oxford Review of Education*, 33 (2), 143–160.

Richardson, W., Woolhouse, J. and Finegold, D. (eds) (1993) *The reform of post-16 education and training in England and Wales*. Harlow: Longman.

Rodger, J., Cowen, G. and Brass, J. (2003) *National evaluation of learning partnerships: Final report*. DfES Research Report RR391. Nottingham: DfES.

Ryan, P. (ed.) (1992) *International comparisons of vocational education and training for intermediate skills*. London: The Falmer Press.

Ryan, P., Gospel, H. and Lewis, P. (2006) Educational and contractual attributes of apprenticeship programmes of large employers in Britain. *Journal of Vocational Education and Training*, 58 (3), 359–383.

Sargant, N. and Aldridge, F. (2002) *Adult learning and social division: A persistent pattern – the full NIACE survey on adult participation in learning 2002* (Volume 1). Leicester: NIACE.

Savory, C., Hodgson, A. and Spours, K. (2003) *The Advanced Vocational Certificate of Education: A general or vocational qualification?* Broadening the Advanced Level Curriculum. IOE/Nuffield Series No. 7. London: Institute of Education, University of London.

Schuller, T., Preston, J., Hammond, C., Brassett-Grundy, A. and Bynner, J. (2004) *The benefits of learning: The impact of education on health, family life and social capital*. London: Routledge Falmer.

Scottish Executive (2004) *A curriculum for excellence: The Curriculum Review Group*. Edinburgh: Scottish Executive.

Secondary Heads Association (SHA) (1994) *14–19 pathways to achievement: A discussion paper*. Leicester: SHA.

Sector Skills Development Agency (SSDA) (2006) *Skills for Business Network 2005: Survey of employers*, research report 18. Wath-upon-Dearne: SSDA.

Shepherd, J. (2008) Diplomas off to a halting start. *Guardian*, 8 Jan.

Smith, P., Kerr, K. and Harris, S. (2003) *Collaboration between independent and local authority schools: LEA's perspectives on partnership and community activities*. Slough: NFER.

Smithers, A. (1994) *All our futures: Britain's education revolution*. A Dispatches report on education, Channel 4 television.

Smithers, A. (2004) A new diploma goes nowhere. *Evening Standard*, 17 Feb.

Spours, K. (1993) 'The reform of qualifications in a divided system' in Richardson, W., Woolhouse, J. and Finegold, D. (eds) *The reform of post-16 education and training in England and Wales*. Harlow: Longman.

Spours, K. (1997) 'GNVQs and the future of broad vocational qualifications' in Hodgson, A. and Spours, K. (eds) *Dearing and beyond: 14–19 curriculum, qualifications and frameworks.* London: Kogan Page.

Spours, K., Coffield, F. and Gregson, M. (2007a) Mediation, translation and local ecologies: understanding the impact of policy levers on further education colleges. *Journal of Vocational Education and Training,* 59 (2), 193–211.

Spours, K., Steer, R. and Hodgson, A. (2007b) *Moving from a learning and skills sector to an equitable, effective and inclusive learning system.* Paper presented at BERA Annual Conference, London, 5–8 Sep. 2007, Institute of Education, University of London.

Stanistreet, P. (2004) A revolution in the air? *Adults Learning,* 16 (4), 8–15.

Stanton, G. (2004) The organisation of full-time 14–19 provision in the state sector. Nuffield Review Working Paper 13. www. nuffield14-19review.org.uk/cgi/documents/documents.cgi?a=30&t=te mplate.htm, accessed 9 Nov. 2007.

Stanton, G. (2005) *National institutional patterns and the effects of these on aspects of participation, attainment and progression,* Discussion Paper 2, Nuffield Review of 14–19 Education and Training. www. nuffield14-19review.org.uk/cgi/documents/documents.cgi?a=137&t=te mplate.htm, accessed 1 Oct. 2007.

Stanton, G. and Bailey, B. (2004) 'Fit for purpose? Sixty years of VET policy in England' in Hayward, G. and James, S. (eds) *Balancing the skills equation: Key issues and challenges for policy and practice.* Bristol: The Policy Press.

Stanton. G. and Fletcher, M. (2006) *14–19 institutional arrangements in England: A research perspective on collaboration, competition and patterns of post-16 provision.* Nuffield Review Working Paper 38. www. nuffield14-19review.org.uk, accessed Aug. 2006.

Stasz, C., Hayward, G., Oh, S. and Wright, S. (2004) *Outcomes and processes in vocational learning: A review of the literature.* London: LSRC.

Steedman, H. (2001) *Benchmarking apprenticeships: UK and continental Europe compared.* Centre for Economic Performance Working Paper. London: London School of Economics.

Steer, R. and Grainger, P. (2007) *Raising Enjoyment and Achievement (REAch) Programme: Findings from a pupil attitudinal survey.* London: Post-14 Centre for Research and Innovation, Institute of Education, University of London.

Stobart, G. (2008) *Testing times: The uses and abuses of assessment.* London: Routledge.

Styles, B., Fletcher, M. and Valentine, R. (2006) *Implementing 14–19 provision: A focus on schools.* London: LSDA.

Taylor (1993) 'TVEI and the curriculum 14–18' in Tomlinson, H. (ed.) *Education and training 14–19: Continuity and diversity in the curriculum.* Harlow: Longman.

Teachernet (2007a) *Increased Flexibility for 14–16 Year Olds Programme.* www.teachernet.gov.uk/teachingandlearning/14to19/collaboration/ifp/, accessed 1 Oct. 2007.

Teachernet (2007b) *Young Apprenticeships.* www.teachernet.gov.uk/teachingandlearning/14to19/vocationaloffer/Apprenticeships/youngapprenticeships/, accessed 1 Oct. 2007.

Tirrell, J., Winter, A. M. and Hawthorne, S. (2006) *Challenges facing partnerships: Current developments towards implementation of 14–19 in local authorities.* Sheffield: LEACAN 14+ Ltd.

Tomlinson, M. (2002a) *Report on outcomes of review of A level grading.* London: DfES.

Tomlinson, M. (2002b) *Enquiry into A level standards: Final report.* London: DfES.

Torrance, H. (2006) *Assessment in post-compulsory education: Paper 4: Assessment as learning? How the uses of explicit learning objectives and assessment criteria can come to dominate learning.* Paper presented to the British Educational Research Association, University of Warwick, 6–9 Sep.

Townsend, M. (2004) A word from the editor. *Sunday Express,* 22 Apr.

UCAS/DfES Curriculum Development Group (2005) *Discussion questions on the 14–19 Education White Paper: Response from the colleges of the University of Cambridge.* Cheltenham: UCAS.

Undy, C. (2007) Budget dismays small businesses. *FSB News Release,* 21 Mar.

Unwin, L. and Ryan, P. (2007) *Incentives for employer involvement.* Paper given at a Nuffield 14–19 Review Seminar, 10 Jul.

Warmington, P., Daniels, H. E., Edwards, A., Leadbetter, J., Martin, D., Brown, S. and Middleton, D. (2004) *Learning in and for interagency working: Conceptual tensions in 'joined up' practice.* Paper presented at ESRC Teaching and Learning Research Programme Conference, Cardiff, Nov.

Welsh Assembly Government (WAG) (2002) *Learning pathways 14–19: Consultation document.* Cardiff: WAG.

Whitbread, N. (1991) 'The Education Reform Act: A missed opportunity for 16+' in Chitty, C. (ed.) *Post-16 education: Studies in access and achievement.* London: Kogan Page.

Whiteside, T. (1992) 'The "alliance" and the shaping of the agenda' in Whiteside, T., Sutton, A. and Everton, T. (eds) *16–19 changes in education and training.* London: David Fulton

Whitty, G. (2002) *Making sense of education policy.* London: Paul Chapman.

Wilde, S. and Wright, S. (2007) On the same wavelength but tuned to different frequencies? Perceptions of academic and administrative staff in England and Wales on the articulation between 14–19 education and training and higher education. *London Review of Education*, 5 (3), 299–312.

Williams, S. (1999) Policy tensions in vocational education and training for young people: the origins of general national vocational education. *Journal of Education Policy*, 14 (2), 151–166.

Wolf, A. (2002) *Does education matter? Myths about education and economic growth.* Harmondsworth: Penguin.

Wolf, A. (2007) *Diminished returns: How raising the leaving age to 18 will harm young people and the economy.* London: Policy Exchange.

Working Group on 14–19 Reform (2003a) *Principles for reform of 14–19 learning programmes and qualifications.* Annersley: DfES.

Working Group on 14–19 Reform (2003b) *Principles for reform of 14–19 learning programmes and qualifications, summary document.* Annersley: DfES.

Working Group on 14–19 Reform (2004a) *14–19 curriculum and qualifications reform: final report of the Working Group.* London: DfES.

Working Group on 14–19 Reform (2004b) *14–19 curriculum and qualifications reform: interim report of the Working Group.* London: DfES.

Young, M. and Leney, T. (1997) 'From A levels to an advanced level curriculum of the future' in Hodgson, A. and Spours, K. (eds) *Dearing and beyond: 14–19 qualifications, frameworks and systems.* London: Kogan Page.

Young, M. F. D. (1998) *The curriculum of the future: From 'new sociology of education' to a critical theory of learning.* London: Routledge/Falmer.

Young, M. F. D. (2008) *Bringing knowledge back in: From social constructivism to social realism in the sociology of education.* London: Routledge.

index